Paul Mallard

Comfort & Hope for Parents of Prodigals

"Is there any area of our lives in which we need comfort and hope more than in our parenting? Paul Mallard gives us sound biblical guidance, practical wisdom, and enough hope to keep praying for our children, whether they are walking with Jesus or not."

REV. DR MICHAEL P. JENSEN, Rector, St Mark's Darling Point, Sydney

"In every congregation, faithful disciples are wrestling with the painful heartache of unbelieving children. With a tender tone but not avoiding difficult topics, Paul Mallard provides faithful pastoral counsel, full of the grace and truth of our Lord Jesus. There is help here not only for parents in pain but also for those seeking to support them, and those who pray for wandering prodigals."

JONATHAN PRIME, Director for London, FIEC

"Paul Mallard has drawn on decades of pastoral experience to provide practical wisdom for parents in pain. Writing with biblical conviction and compassionate understanding, Paul addresses the problems parents of prodigals face and the questions they ask. Highlights for me include Paul's application of 1 Corinthians 13 to loving rebellious children; his ten ways to pray for unconverted loved ones; his exhortation that 'we must not let our unsaved children drive a wedge between ourselves and our spouses'; his counsel on relating to loved ones who experience same-sex attraction and gender confusion; and his affirmation that the strong bond of parental love is a reflection of the love of God, which never lets his people go. I was helped by reading this book and quickly thought of others to whom I'd like to pass it on. I expect you will find the same."

COLIN S. SMITH, Pastor Emeritus, The Orchard; President, Open the Bible (openthebible.org)

"As a redeemed prodigal and now a parent myself, I found Paul's words to be grace-filled, practically helpful and full of hope. Regardless of the stage of life, *When Children Walk Away* will spur on and encourage every Christian parent longing to see their child's life redeemed by the power of Jesus."

SARAH WALTON, Co-author, *Hope When it Hurts;*
Author, *The Long Road Home*

"Every now and again, a book is written which makes me think to myself, 'Why wasn't this written years ago?' This is one of those. It's a subject that is constantly relevant because it's a topic that is always painful, difficult, distressing and confusing. Paul writes with a pastor's loving wisdom, a preacher's clear communication and a theologian's faithful understanding. Every church member is going to benefit from this volume: it's for those directly affected by the sadness of unbelieving children and grandchildren; and it's for every believer as we stand with hurting brothers and sisters. Above all, while grounded in biblical reality, Paul offers us all hope: 'The arm of the LORD is not too short to save' (Isaiah 59:1)."

ADRIAN REYNOLDS, Pastor; Author; father and grandfather;
Associate National Director, Fellowship of Independent
Evangelical Churches, UK

I would like to thank Marjie Hutchinson, Hilary Jackson, Howard Jackson, Daryl Jones and Don Morrison.

Thank you for your help in preparing this book.

Thank you for reading the manuscript and for your wise and insightful comments.

When Children Walk Away from Jesus

Published by:
The Good Book Company

thegoodbook.com | thegoodbook.co.uk
thegoodbook.com.au | thegoodbook.co.nz

Every book published by The Good Book Company has been written by a human author and edited by a human editor. While AI tools are sometimes used to assist with research and support certain processes, all content has been created by a human author and thoroughly checked by our editorial team to ensure it is biblically faithful and pastorally wise.

Cover design by Faceout Studio | Art direction and design by André Parker

ISBN: 9781802543766 | JOB-008455 | Printed in India

CONTENTS

Introduction 9

1. Why Does It Hurt So Much? 13
2. What Is My Child's Greatest Need? 27
3. Where Did We Go Wrong? 41
4. Does God Promise to Save Our Children? 53
5. What Should We Pray? 67
6. How Do We Show Love to Our Unsaved Children? 79
7. Am I Still Allowed to Love Him? 93
8. Can I Grow Through the Pain? 113
9. What About...? 127
10. How Can We Help? 139

Epilogue 151

INTRODUCTION

Rick and Julie have three children.* They all grew up in the same home with the same Christian atmosphere. They all went to the same school, the same church youth group and the same Christian camps. All three of them professed faith and were baptised in their late teens. But now the contrast could not be starker. One of their sons is following Christ and serves in the church; their daughter attends church but is only nominal in her faith; their second son has drifted away from the faith entirely and lives with his girlfriend.

How do you explain the difference?

Rachel is a single mum. Her journey to faith started when she brought her son Daniel to a local church's parent-and-toddler group. They began attending services on Sundays, and Rachel was saved. Daniel also professed faith and, at the age of 19, went off to Bible college to train as a youth pastor. Rachel and all her friends at church were

---

* In this book I will use a number of illustrations from the personal experience of parents in pain. In each case I have their permission, but I have changed their names.

thrilled. He finished his course and got his first job. And then, out of the blue, he announced to his mum that he had lost his faith. It was just a fairy story, and Christians were hypocrites.

What went wrong?

George and Stella have a daughter called Kate. She seemed a happy little girl, but when she started high school, things fell apart. She was bullied and eventually developed an eating disorder. People at church prayed for her, but it seemed to get worse. After school she went through a series of toxic relationships. One day she told her parents that she was a lesbian. She said that if they didn't affirm her chosen life, she didn't want anything more to do with them. They pleaded with her, trying to find a way to maintain the relationship, but she was adamant. At the time of writing, George and Stella have not seen Kate for over two years.

How could this happen?

Having spent 40 years as a pastor, I could tell you many stories of children who were brought up in a Christian home and are now following Christ wholeheartedly.

But this book is not about those kinds of children.

It's about the other type of story I've seen play out. This book is for parents with children who were brought up in a Christian home but have since walked away from Jesus. Sometimes their rejection of Christianity happens suddenly and dramatically. In other cases, it's a gradual drift over many years. In either case, it's heartbreaking.

This may be your family's story. If it isn't, you will certainly know someone for whom this is a continuous source of crippling pain. For every family where the children seem to be well established in the faith, there will be another where one or more of the children have deserted it. In most cases, the relationship between parents and children functions pretty well—the children respect, love and care for Mum and Dad. But they've tasted Christianity first-hand and want little or nothing more to do with it.

Who is this book for?

It is for you if you are experiencing the pain of a unsaved child.

It is for you if you are watching someone go through this.

It is for you if you want to minister to prodigals, their parents and their grandparents.

It is for you if you are afraid of losing your children.

It is written to help you to find grace and hope in loving children who do not love Jesus.

CHAPTER 1

WHY DOES IT HURT SO MUCH?

Joy... and Pain

One of the great joys of pastoral ministry is that you often get to visit new parents when their child has just been born. It can be very revealing. The moment that the midwife puts that tiny squalling cosmos into their arms, they know that things will never be the same again.

I think, for example, of a huge rugby player I knew, who was built like a refrigerator, gently cradling his newborn daughter and staring into her upturned face. I looked at him as he looked at her and thought, "The poor bloke has had it! He has just fallen in love. And nothing will ever be the same again."

Or there was the couple who had been married for 20 years and never thought that this would happen. After so many disappointments, they finally got the unexpected gift of a child. They looked as if they would explode with joy.

> *We had accepted that this would never happen and were determined to find all our satisfaction in the Lord. And then he surprised us! We are the most blessed people in the world! And at the same time, it's terrifying!*

Our children are one of the greatest gifts that God can place into our hands. They are a joy and a delight and a privilege. But at the same time, the responsibility can seem overwhelming. That's why it can be terrifying. What if we get it wrong?

And sometimes our worst fear is realised. The children we cherished from before the first breath was in their lungs have rejected Christ and show no signs of ever returning to him.

So, along with the joy, parenthood can bring the most excruciating pain. You cannot love someone without opening yourself to injury. Love makes us vulnerable, and the more we love, the more we suffer. Grief is the price we pay for love.

And there is no pain like parental pain. A foolish child will break your heart. The Bible warns us as much.

Wise and Foolish Children

King Solomon was the wisest man of his time. The book of Proverbs records his God-given wisdom. After a series of profound meditations on the nature of wisdom (1 – 9), he begins a long list of individual wise sayings (10:1 – 22:16). At the head of the list, we find these words:

> *A wise son brings joy to his father,*
> *but a foolish son brings grief to his mother. (10:1)*

Solomon speaks about sons, but it applies to daughters too. The contrast is stark—our children can be wise or foolish, and this will bring us either joy or grief.

Wisdom must not be confused with intelligence. Someone can have a very high IQ and yet behave like a fool. It is similarly possible to have few paper qualifications and yet to live a profoundly wise life. The secret of wisdom is the fear of the Lord:

> *The fear of the LORD is the beginning of knowledge,*
> *but fools despise wisdom and instruction.* (1:7)

This verse acts as a kind of motto text for the whole book, from chapter 1 to the end (31:31). So what does it mean to fear the Lord? Fearing God goes hand in hand with loving and trusting him. We can enjoy and delight in God while treating him with reverence and awe. We can call him our Father, but we must remember that, in the words of the Lord's Prayer, our Father is "in heaven"—exalted far beyond us. Our greatest concern must be that his name is hallowed, his kingdom is established and his will is done.

Solomon says that a wise child will fear God and bring joy to his parents. Submitting to their instruction, he or she will successfully negotiate their way through the temptations of this world, whether they be dishonest gain (1:10-19) or sexual immorality (2:16-18). But a foolish child who turns their heart away from God will bring grief.

This is such an important warning that Solomon repeats it several times:

> *To have a fool for a child brings grief;*
> *there is no joy for the parent of a godless fool.* (17:21)

A foolish son brings grief to his father
and bitterness to the mother who bore him. (v 25)

On occasions we find the anxious parent stepping off the pages of the book to appeal to their child:

My son, if your heart is wise,
then my heart will be glad indeed;
my inmost being will rejoice
when your lips speak what is right. (23:15-16)

So a foolish child is one who rejects godly parental guidance and does not fear the Lord. A child can be foolish in all sorts of ways, but the most foolish thing that any child can do is to reject Jesus Christ. We may have all sorts of aspirations for our children, but surely our greatest longing is that they might come to know the Saviour. When they turn their back on him, it feels like a sword to the heart.

And this foolishness can take many forms.

A Wide Spectrum

Sometimes this foolishness is easy to spot.

Our children may get in trouble with the law or pursue destructive behaviours such as bulimia or self-harm. Their actions may have grave consequences—an unwanted pregnancy or a failed marriage. There may be the harmful effects of addiction or substance abuse. Perhaps you're having to watch as your child embraces a lifestyle of sexual promiscuity or same-sex relationships or gender confusion.

Jesus' famous parable of the prodigal son gives us a picture of this kind of out-and-out rebellion (Luke 15:11-32).

> *There was a man who had two sons. The younger one said to his father, "Father, give me my share of the estate." So he divided his property between them. (v 11)*

The younger son does not want to spend his inheritance in philanthropic projects but in self-indulgent adventures. He is often referred to as *prodigal* because he behaved in an extravagant way (which is what the word actually means). He is wasteful, reckless, imprudent and immoderate. Eventually he loses everything and ends up with the pigs. Here he comes to his senses:

> *"How many of my father's hired servants have food to spare, and here I am starving to death! I will set out and go back to my father and say to him: Father, I have sinned against heaven and against you. I am no longer worthy to be called your son; make me like one of your hired servants." So he got up and went to his father.*
>
> *(v 17-20)*

On returning home, he is barely able to utter his words of repentance before his father embraces him and celebrates his return.

> *But the father said to his servants, "Quick! Bring the best robe and put it on him. Put a ring on his finger and sandals on his feet. Bring the fattened calf and kill it. Let's have a feast and celebrate. For this son of mine was dead and is alive again; he was lost and is found." So they began to celebrate. (v 22-24)*

We may think that this is a fitting conclusion to the story. But we have forgotten the second son. And he is just as much a rebel against his father—but in a different way.

When he hears about the celebration, he is furious and refuses to join in, castigating his father:

> *Look! All these years I've been slaving for you and never disobeyed your orders. Yet you never gave me even a young goat so I could celebrate with my friends. But when this son of yours who has squandered your property with prostitutes comes home, you kill the fattened calf for him! (v 29-30)*

Perhaps we feel some sympathy. But the father sees more clearly than his older son:

> *"My son," the father said, "you are always with me, and everything I have is yours. But we had to celebrate and be glad, because this brother of yours was dead and is alive again; he was lost and is found." (v 31-32)*

Jesus is teaching against the backdrop of the angry murmuring of the religious leaders who are scandalised by his acceptance of sinful people at his table (v 1-2). The two sons—like the religious leaders and the sinful outcasts of Jesus' day—stand at two ends of a spectrum.

The first son cast off parental guidance, wasted his material possessions, and might have lost his life in the process. He scorned the precious relationship with his father. He was destitute economically, socially and spiritually. The second son worked tirelessly in the family business, but he also rejected his father's values. By his attitude of heart and refusal to forgive, he showed that he despised his father's grace and kindness. Both boys bring grief to their father.

This parable illustrates the wide spectrum of ways in which an unbelieving child may distance themselves from their parents—and ultimately from God himself, whom the father in the story represents.

At one end of the spectrum is the child who rejects both their parents' faith and their parents' values. This may be caused by some terrifying and life-destroying addiction. Or the fractures in the relationship may be because of lifestyle choices that are acceptable in the world's eyes but not in the Lord's. Sometimes the alienation seems to have no obvious root cause, but the child simply drifts away from the parent over time. Contact becomes rare or non-existent.

At the other end of the spectrum, there is the "respectable" child who stays close to their parents and shows them great honour. Perhaps they attend church and encourage their own children to be part of a Christian community. They have good marriages and fruitful careers. They may even share many of the beliefs of their parents. I knew one young man who was convinced by the "young earth" account of creation—that God created the world in six literal days. Even when studying physics at university, he refused to abandon this position. But he openly confessed that he was not a Christian. He was convinced of the truthfulness of the Christian faith but had no personal trust in Jesus. And this is the crux of the matter. It is possible to say all the right things and to behave in a respectable, almost "Christian" way, and yet be unsaved.

And of course there is a wide range of experience that sit somewhere in between. Where does your child fall on this spectrum?

If your child is more towards the *respectable* end, the temptation is complacency. They may be happy and well. They may seem like good people. But they still need Jesus.

If your child is in open rebellion, the temptation is to despair. But don't give up. No one is so far gone that they are outside the orbit of God's grace. He is more than capable of running out to meet them and welcoming them home.

We'll say more about both of these temptations later. But first it's important to acknowledge that wherever your child lies on the spectrum, an appropriate response to their lostness is grief.

Kids Break Your Heart

The word translated "grief" in Proverbs 10:1 refers to extreme emotional pain—akin to the pain of bereavement.

Think of the grief of King David. His rebellious son, Absalom, endangers his father's life and tries to snatch the kingdom from him. But when David hears that Absalom has been killed in the battle, he is overcome with grief.

> *The king was shaken. He went up to the room over the gateway and wept. As he went, he said: "O my son Absalom! My son, my son Absalom! If only I had died instead of you—O Absalom, my son, my son!"*
>
> *(2 Samuel 18:33)*

If we read on into the next chapter of 2 Samuel, we discover that this grief is so overwhelming that it causes David to lose all perspective. He neglects his kingly responsibilities as sorrow smothers his heart. Joab, the commander of his army, is driven to warn David:

> *Now go out and encourage your men. I swear by the* L*ORD* *that if you don't go out, not a man will be left*

> *with you by nightfall. This will be worse for you than all the calamities that have come on you from your youth till now. (19:7)*

In David's case, the death of Absalom meant that there was no hope of restoration. If our children are still alive, we must never abandon hope. One of the purposes of this book is to engender such hope. However, we must also be honest about the reality of the pain which we feel. It is a kind of bereavement.

The word *bereave* comes from an Old English word meaning "to deprive of, to take away by violence, to seize, to rob". When your children walk away from Jesus, it feels as though something precious has been taken away from you. You have invested so much in their upbringing. When you first became a parent, you didn't realise just how demanding it would be, but you raised your children with all the grace, grit and gumption you could muster. You did your best to guard your home and protect your children. You sought to prepare them for the future and for the time when they would leave you and launch out on their own. You wanted them to have roots and wings. You longed for them to live wise and God-honouring lives.

Perhaps it came as a huge shock, then, when these delightful children turned into rebellious teenagers. When they rejected your faith, you experienced both deep pain and a debilitating sense of failure. We may know in theory that all of us are born with a sinful heart and need to experience God's grace personally—but when *our* kids don't come to faith, we often blame ourselves. A sense of failure is one of the constant companions of parenting. We will return to this in chapter 3.

But there's one way this swirl of parental love and grief can also strangely encourage us.

The Gravity of Love

When my kids were small, they loved playing on what they called the death-slide at the indoor soft play centre. You know the kind of thing I mean—a slide with a near vertical drop. You sit on the edge looking down, trying to pluck up the courage to go over the top. But if you get too close, gravity takes over and down you go. There is no arguing with gravity.

There is a kind of gravity about parental love which you only discover when you become a parent. Of course our children love us, but the love that we have for them is usually more profound and sacrificial. We often don't really appreciate the sacrifices that our own parents made for us until we become parents ourselves. Our children may disappoint us and neglect us and break our hearts, and we will still go on loving them. The pull towards them is like gravity. The author Max Lucado captures this in a powerful story about a mother and daughter:

> *Longing to leave her poor Brazilian neighbourhood, Christina wanted to see the world. Discontent with a home having only a pallet on the floor, a washbasin, and a wood-burning stove, she dreamed of a better life in the city. One morning she slipped away, breaking her mother's heart. Knowing what life on the streets would be like for her young, attractive daughter, Maria hurriedly packed to go find her. On her way to the bus stop she entered a drugstore to get one last thing. Pictures. She sat*

in the photograph booth, closed the curtain, and spent all she could on pictures of herself. With her purse full of small black-and-white photos, she boarded the next bus to Rio de Janeiro. Maria knew Christina had no way of earning money. She also knew that her daughter was too stubborn to give up. When pride meets hunger, a human will do things that were before unthinkable. Knowing this, Maria began her search. Bars, hotels, nightclubs, any place with the reputation for street walkers or prostitutes. She went to them all. And at each place she left her picture—taped on a bathroom mirror, tacked to a hotel bulletin board, fastened to a corner phone booth. And on the back of each photo she wrote a note.

It wasn't too long before both the money and the pictures ran out, and Maria had to go home. The weary mother wept as the bus began its long journey back to her small village. It was a few weeks later that young Christina descended the hotel stairs. Her young face was tired. Her brown eyes no longer danced with youth but spoke of pain and fear. Her laughter was broken. Her dream had become a nightmare. A thousand times over she had longed to trade these countless beds for her secure pallet. Yet the little village was, in too many ways, too far away. As she reached the bottom of the stairs, her eyes noticed a familiar face. She looked again, and there on the lobby mirror was a small picture of her mother. Christina's eyes burned and her throat tightened as she walked across the room and removed the small photo. Written on the back was this compelling invitation. "Whatever you have done, whatever you have become, it doesn't matter. Please come home." She did.[1]

I can't help but hear an echo of the story of the prodigal son. As we reflect on the gravity of a parent's love, perhaps we can enter the heart of God. Our love for our children gives us a glimpse of his love for us—which is greater by far.

The prophet Hosea compares God's love to the love of a father, with the nation of Israel being his rebellious son. The Lord says:

When Israel was a child, I loved him,
and out of Egypt I called my son.
But the more they were called,
the more they went away from me.
They sacrificed to the Baals
and they burned incense to images.
It was I who taught Ephraim to walk,
taking them by the arms;
but they did not realise
it was I who healed them.
I led them with cords of human kindness,
with ties of love.
To them I was like one who lifts
a little child to the cheek,
and I bent down to feed them. (Hosea 11:1-4)

Can you feel the tenderness of God's love here? Hosea deliberately uses images which reflect the affection and compassion God has for his people.

Because of Israel's sin, the Lord must chasten the rebellious nation. But he cannot stop loving his son:

How can I give you up, Ephraim?
How can I hand you over, Israel?
How can I treat you like Admah?

> *How can I make you like Zeboyim?*
> *My heart is changed within me;*
> *all my compassion is aroused.*
> *I will not carry out my fierce anger,*
> *nor will I devastate Ephraim again.*
> *For I am God, and not a man—*
> *the Holy One among you.*
> *I will not come against their cities. (v 8-9)*

When we love our wayward children, we are experiencing something of God's heart towards us. The Lord set up human families for this very purpose—to show us something true about him. Parental love—however costly—is a beautiful God-given gift.

QUESTIONS

1. Do you think your wayward child is more like the younger son or the older son, or somewhere in between?

2. This chapter touched on lots of different things we might be feeling: complacency, despair, grief, pain, shock, hope, love. Which of those best describe the way that you're feeling at the moment with regard to your unbelieving child? How have your feelings changed over time?

3. What do you think it would look like to "feel rightly" in this situation?

4. In what ways have you experienced the gravity of parental love? How does it give you an insight into the heart of God?

CHAPTER 2

WHAT IS MY CHILD'S GREATEST NEED?

The Wrath of the Lamb

I was converted when I was eleven years old. After my conversion, my first great concern was the salvation of my parents. I loved my mum and dad, and they were brilliant parents. When I told them that I had become a Christian, they never put any barriers in my way—but they did make it clear that they were not interested in following Jesus. I started praying for them every day.

Matters came to a head when I went off to university. I had never been away from home before and felt homesick. It also focused my mind and heart on the fact that my mum and dad were going to hell. When it began to affect my work, I spoke to my tutor, and he directed me to talk to the chaplain in my college.

The chaplain listened to me sympathetically and then spoke soothingly:

> *I think you are torturing yourself unnecessarily. Your parents sound like wonderful people. There may be a place called hell, although I doubt it. But one thing you can be sure of is that your mum and dad won't be there. The Jesus I know wouldn't send nice people to hell.*

But this is not what the Bible says. It is quite clear about both the reality of hell and the lostness of those who die without faith in Christ. One of the most terrifying passages in the Bible describes the final judgment like this:

> *Then the kings of the earth, the princes, the generals, the rich, the mighty, and everyone else, both slave and free, hid in caves and among the rocks of the mountains. They called to the mountains and the rocks, "Fall on us and hide us from the face of him who sits on the throne and from the wrath of the Lamb! For the great day of their wrath has come, and who can withstand it?"*
>
> *(Revelation 6:15-17)*

Notice that this judgment is universal—encompassing people from every walk of life. It is terrifying because there is nothing on the day of judgment to hide lost people from the wrath of God and of the Lamb. Jesus is the Lamb of God, who takes away the sin of the world (John 1:29). But those who fail to take refuge in him will one day face his wrath.

But the question is: Do we really believe that? Do we really believe that without Christ our children are lost?

The biblical doctrine of hell is emotionally draining and intellectually challenging. Many today, like that chaplain, dismiss it as a relic of the past. Or perhaps you just quietly hope that it isn't as bad as all that. You cling to the thought that come judgment day, God might be merciful. Or you hope for last-minute deathbed conversions. Or you simply do your best not to think about hell at all.

It's not my purpose here to dwell on the subject in an unhealthy way. However, if we are to be faithful to the Bible, and in particular to the teaching of Jesus, we cannot ignore the seriousness with which it addresses eternal matters.

So in this chapter, I'm going to invite you to take a deep breath, ask God for courage, and look with me at those teachings, full-on in the face. After all, above everything else that we want for our children, we should want them to be saved. For what is the advantage if they gain the whole world and lose their souls (Mark 8:36)?

The Three "R"s

It used to be quite common to talk about "the three Rs"—the three basic skills taught in school—of reading, writing and arithmetic. (Granted, only one of them starts with R!) Apparently one of the first references to these three skills came in the writings of the 5th-century Christian theologian Augustine. He alludes to them in his autobiographical book *Confessions.*[2]

Later on I discovered that Augustine's theology was marked out by another three Rs—ruin, redemption and regeneration. If we are to correctly diagnose what our children most need, we must be convinced of the reality of these three important theological words.

RUIN

It is very easy to be sentimental in our view of children. I have nine grandchildren, and they are a constant joy to me.

One of the blessings of being a grandparent is that you have all the fun without much responsibility! Each grandchild is unique. Each one is a delight. And they are all good kids. I love them to bits.

But the Bible tells me quite clearly that they are lost sinners, who need to be reconciled to God. For all of our seeming "innocence", every one of us is born with a sinful heart. This does not mean that we are as sinful as we could possibly be or that we have lost the ability to distinguish between good and evil. What it does mean is that none of us are free from sin and that it affects every part of our lives.

Sin runs deep. It stems right from the heart, which, according to the Bible, is the driving force behind our whole character:

> *The heart is deceitful above all things and beyond cure. Who can understand it? (Jeremiah 17:9)*

> *For it is from within, out of a person's heart, that evil thoughts come—sexual immorality, theft, murder, adultery, greed, malice, deceit, lewdness, envy, slander, arrogance and folly. All these evils come from inside and defile a person. (Mark 7:21-23)*

Because the heart has been corrupted, our thinking has been darkened, our will has been enslaved, our conscience has been desensitized and our desires have been distorted. We are ruined. Paul describes our pre-conversion state like this:

> *All of us also lived among [the disobedient] at one time, gratifying the cravings of our flesh and following its desires and thoughts. Like the rest, we were by nature deserving of wrath. (Ephesians 2:3)*

Although human beings retain the image of God and therefore have a unique dignity that sets us apart from the rest of God's creation, every one of us, including our children, are members of a fallen race. The 17th-century mathematician and philosopher Blaise Pascal put it like this:

> *What a chimera then is man! What a novelty, what a monster, what a chaos, what a contradiction, what a prodigy! Judge of all things, feeble earthworm, repository of truth, sewer of uncertainty and error, the glory and scum of the universe.*[3]

This is the enigma of humanity, and we soon come to see it in our children. I have yet to meet the parent who tells me that their son or daughter is so good that they occasionally need to teach them to be naughty so that they can be normal!

The Bible tells us to expect this. In a moment of insight, after his terrible sin with Bathsheba, King David came to recognise the reality of his ruin:

> *Surely I was sinful at birth,*
> *sinful from the time my mother conceived me.*
>
> *(Psalm 51:5)*

No matter how cute or adorable our little children appear, their hearts are out of tune with the heart of God. And no matter how kind or generous or loyal our grown-up children are, they too are spiritually ruined. We may think to ourselves, "Are they really that bad?" But to say otherwise is to call God a liar. The Bible affirms that for all their good qualities, they are living in God's world without reference to its Creator. We fool ourselves when we fail to see that our children are spiritually ruined—and desperately in need of redemption.

REDEMPTION

Once we have accepted the Bible's diagnosis of the human condition, we can begin to appreciate the solution which God has provided. At the heart of the gospel is the death and resurrection of Jesus Christ. This is God's gracious and unmerited solution for ruined men and women.

Earlier in this chapter, we quoted from John's description of the final judgment in Revelation 6. But does this mean that every human being is doomed? Is there any way that we can escape the wrath of the Lamb? John answers these questions in the next chapter of Revelation:

> *After this I looked, and there before me was a great multitude that no one could count, from every nation, tribe, people and language, standing before the throne and before the Lamb. They were wearing white robes and were holding palm branches in their hands.*
>
> *And they cried out in a loud voice:*
>
> *"Salvation belongs to our God, who sits on the throne,*
> *and to the Lamb." (7:9-10)*

This great crowd is a cosmopolitan gathering of people from every culture and every nation. The white robes suggest celebration and purity while the palm branches signify victory and festivity. Later these people are described as those who…

> *… are before the throne of God*
> *and serve him day and night in his temple;*

and he who sits on the throne
will shelter them with his presence. (v 15)

They are enjoying God's presence in heaven. But how did they get there? How can ruined people gain a perfect heaven? How can unholy people shelter in the presence of he holy God? How can unforgiven people enjoy a place where sin is absent?

Perhaps these questions are in John's mind when one of the heavenly beings asks him:

These in white robes—who are they, and where did they come from? (v 13)

John confesses his ignorance and receives the answer:

These are they who have come out of the great tribulation; they have washed their robes and made them white in the blood of the Lamb. (v 14)

This great multitude may have experienced tribulation and suffering in this world, but now all their trials are over.

"Never again will they hunger;
never again will they thirst.
The sun will not beat down on them,"
nor any scorching heat.
For the Lamb at the centre of the throne
will be their shepherd;
"he will lead them to springs of living water."
"And God will wipe away every tear from their eyes."
(v 16-17)

This is a wonderful picture of the glory and intimacy of heaven. But the passage is also very specific. They did not earn their place before the throne. They did not get there on merit. It wasn't because they were "good kids" who honoured their father and mother and tried hard to please God.

They are redeemed and in heaven because they have been made clean by the blood of the Lamb. It was because of his perfect life and substitutionary death that they are now enjoying the Lamb for ever.

Redemption is the work of Christ on our behalf, whereby he ransoms us, at the price of his own life, securing our deliverance from the bondage and condemnation of sin. God has redeemed us through the blood of his Son and "rescued us from the dominion of darkness and brought us into the kingdom of the Son he loves, in whom we have redemption, the forgiveness of sins" (Colossians 1:13-14).

On the cross Jesus bore the punishment for the guilt of all the sins we have committed and has "redeemed us from the curse of the law by becoming a curse for us" (Galatians 3:13).

We must never undervalue the cost of this redemption:

> *It was not with perishable things such as silver or gold that you were redeemed from the empty way of life handed down to you from your ancestors, but with the precious blood of Christ, a lamb without blemish or defect. (1 Peter 1:18-19)*

Forgiveness is only ours through faith. And only those who have been forgiven and been made clean by the blood of Christ will go to heaven. Our children are no exception.

If we want our children to become Christians, we need to make much of the cross. When I became a Christian at the age of eleven, it was the cross of Christ that drew me. I didn't make a neat little decision on the basis of logic—I fled to the cross for salvation. Even if your children have strayed far from the faith, you can assure them that the blood of Christ is sufficient to cover all their sins. God specialises in saving rebels.

The cross gives us hope.

REGENERATION

If my children are spiritually dead, then what they need is spiritual life. They need nothing less than a miracle.

I think that's what dawned on me in my first term at university. One morning I was reading the book of Ephesians as part of my personal devotions, and I got to the second chapter:

> *As for you, you were dead in your transgressions and sins… (Ephesians 2:1)*

It hit me like a freight train. Paul's diagnosis is stark. We are not just spiritually sick or disabled. We are spiritually dead. We don't need a doctor; we need a miracle. We need to be born again.

Jesus made this clear in his dialogue with Nicodemus (John 3:1-18).

Nicodemus was the ultimate establishment figure. He was a Pharisee, a member of the Jewish ruling council and one of the leading theologians in Israel (v 1, 10). His mum and dad were probably very proud of him! He had been impressed by Jesus' miraculous signs and was puzzling over his identity. Could he be the Messiah? In response to his unasked questions, Jesus told him this:

> *Very truly I tell you, no one can see the kingdom of God unless they are born again. (v 3)*

Nicodemus is religious and highly admired but is spiritually blind and dead. His grasp of theology, his dedication to religion and his unblemished respectability will not get him to heaven. He needs to be born again or, more literally, "born from above". He needs God to reach into his life and to transform him. Theologians refer to this as *regeneration*. This is a miraculous act of the Holy Spirit, in which he grants spiritual life to a dead soul. Nicodemus should have understood this because it was predicted by the prophet Ezekiel:

> *I will give you a new heart and put a new spirit in you; I will remove from you your heart of stone and give you a heart of flesh. And I will put my Spirit in you and move you to follow my decrees and be careful to keep my laws.*
> *(Ezekiel 36:26-27)*

When we hear of some remarkable conversion story, the idea of new birth seems obvious. But Nicodemus was a pillar of the religious establishment who should have had a fine grasp of theology. And yet he still needed what is equivalent to a spiritual resurrection.

And our children are the same. They may have grown up in the church. They may have recited the memory verses, sung the songs, and won all the trivia quizzes in Sunday school. They may have given the appearance of life at one stage—but without God's intervention, they remain spiritually dead. They need a spiritual resurrection.

The Greatest Need

Let's return to the question of this chapter's title: what is your child's greatest need?

When our unsaved children really go off the rails, we are tempted to think that their biggest problem is addiction or sexual confusion or a broken marriage or an unwanted pregnancy. All of these things will cause heartache. But in the end they are only symptoms. The underlying need is for salvation. It is easy to concentrate on externals, but their real problem is that they don't see Jesus clearly. Pray for them to be converted and not just that they would become "good kids".

On the other hand, our unsaved children may be wonderfully "respectable". They may work hard, love their families and honour their parents. They may even attend church with you on high days and holidays. They don't openly attack the Christian faith, but they have walked away from God and are not interested in going back. They still need Jesus and are lost without him. The best thing you can do for such children is to show them Jesus so that they are captivated by his love and satisfied with him alone.

No one is too difficult for God. How easily we put people into categories! We imagine that it is easier for God with *this* person but that God will have real problems with *that* person. And maybe we do that with our children as well. We think that "this one is too wayward". Or "that one is so happy and successful that they'll never sense their spiritual need". But God is able to woo and win any heart, including the hardened heart of your wayward child.

Listen to the words of Jesus:

> *All those the Father gives me will come to me, and whoever comes to me I will never drive away.*
>
> *(John 6:37)*

And the words of Paul:

> *For those God foreknew he also predestined to be conformed to the image of his Son, that he might be the firstborn among many brothers and sisters. And those he predestined, he also called; those he called, he also justified; those he justified, he also glorified.*
>
> (Roman 8:29-30)

Your grief is very real, but don't give up. Persist in prayer. God may surprise you.

But even when we accept these great gospel truths, we may still be in a state of emotional turmoil when our children continue to be prodigals. We find ourselves asking questions like "Why do I feel so guilty?" or "Where did we go wrong?"

It is to these questions that we will turn in the next chapter.

QUESTIONS

1. "The biblical doctrine of hell is emotionally draining and intellectually challenging." Did you identify with any of the attempts to minimise or ignore it mentioned in that paragraph?
2. We often speak about the innocence of children. In what ways are they innocent, and in what ways are they not?
3. "If we want our children to become Christians, we need to make much of the cross." What might it look like for you to make much of the cross to your children?
4. What challenges and encouragements can you find in this chapter?

CHAPTER 3

WHERE DID WE GO WRONG?

Is It My Fault?

Marvin and Yolanda wanted to talk. They were regular hard-working members of the congregation, but as they came into the room, it was clear that they were in distress. They got straight to the point:

> *Last week Josh came to see us. It was obvious that he had something on his mind. He told us that he's decided that he's no longer a Christian. He isn't interested in pretending any more.*

Josh was their son. I had baptised him before he went off to university, and he had joined the Christian Union and in his second year had been involved in running a mission. He had even talked to me about the possibility of coming to work in the church as a ministry apprentice.

After leaving university, Josh had moved away and started dating a Christian girl. The relationship hadn't worked out, and he'd gone through a period of depression. His parents were worried, but they never suspected that it had affected his Christian faith.

As they talked with me, it was obvious that they were in the grip of some very strong, negative emotions. There was a sense of shock and fear as well as disappointment and grief. But the overwhelming emotion was guilt.

> *Why didn't we see it coming? How could we have been so blind? Were we so busy at church that we missed what was under our noses? Where did we go wrong?*

We opened the Bible together, talked at some length and prayed. But Marvin and Yolanda could not get beyond the overwhelming sense of personal failure. "If Josh has really departed from the faith, then it's our fault."

Perhaps you are wrestling with the same sense of failure.

When you held your newborn child for the first time, you were filled with a sense of excitement and fear. You read books on parenting. You asked for advice from older Christians. You wanted to get it right. Perhaps your underlying assumption was that if you *did* get it right, then your child would become a Christian. But what if, after all your efforts, all your prayers and all your tears, your child grows up to reject the Saviour you love and follow?

So many parents I've spoken to are left asking, "Where did we go wrong?"

Framing the Question

There are two things worth saying before we go any further. The first regards the relationship between human responsibility and God's actions.

On the one hand, we must avoid the idea that our child's salvation depends on what we do. Some children are saved in the absence of good Christian parenting, while in many a believing family, some children are saved but their brother or sister is not. God is able to save our children even if we get it wrong. So we should avoid thinking, *It's all on me, so I need to do everything.*

On the other hand, the Bible gives clear guidelines about the responsibilities of parents for a reason. How we implement these is often left to wisdom, and Christians will disagree on exactly what this looks like in any given area. But there are clear directions to guide us. We should follow these principles in faith, trusting that in his grace God will do what only he can do. We must not retreat into a kind of fatalism which ignores the means that God uses to bring people to faith. We should avoid thinking, *It's all on God, so I don't need to do anything.*

Second, in this area of the Christian life, as in any area, if we feel guilty, we need to examine ourselves to see if that guilt is right and proper—leading us to repent. On the other hand, it may be the false condemnation of the enemy, who loves to tie us up with unjustified feelings of guilt. So in order to resolve our guilt, we need to know what exactly we were responsible for as parents so we can see whether and in what ways we might have failed. Having done this, we can then move forward in repentance and freedom.

Bring Up a Child...

There are four responsibilities which God gives to Christian parents as they bring up their children.

First, we are to teach our children the word of God. Moses instructed God's people to teach their children to love God and obey his commands:

> *Hear, O Israel: the LORD our God, the LORD is one. Love the LORD your God with all your heart and with all your soul and with all your strength. These commandments that I give you today are to be on your hearts. Impress them on your children. Talk about them when you sit at home and when you walk along the road, when you lie down and when you get up. Tie them as symbols on your hands and bind them on your foreheads.*
>
> *(Deuteronomy 6:4-8)*

The Bible is not just for Sunday. Nor can this be left to Sunday school teachers. It should be the most natural thing in the world for families to talk about God and his word in the normal experiences of life, like sitting at home or going for a walk or going to bed or getting up in the morning. In this way, the celebration of God's goodness and his mighty deeds flows down from one generation to the next:

> *One generation commends your works to another; they tell of your mighty acts. (Psalm 145:4)*

Second, as parents we are to set a good example for our children. My children need to see that I'm not a hypocrite. Our children are watching us, and they can sniff out insincerity a mile off. Do our lives back up our words (James 1:22-24)? They might *hear* me talking about my love for Christ, but do they *see* that my real priority in life is material possessions or self-indulgent pleasures? Do I go to pieces when I face a crisis, or do I model trust in God?

Do my children overhear me speaking disparagingly about other Christians? Some of Jesus' severest warnings are to those who cause little ones to stumble (Matthew 18:6, meaning any believer who is weak in some way). When it comes to teaching our children how to live, what we show is more important than what we say.

Third, we are to discipline our children and direct them in the way in which they should go.

> *Discipline your children, and they will give you peace;*
> *they will bring you the delights you desire.*
> *(Proverbs 29:17)*

Paul puts it like this:

> *Fathers, do not exasperate your children; instead, bring them up in the training and instruction of the Lord."*
> *(Ephesians 6:4)*

In the Roman world, the father had absolute authority. (He could sell his child into slavery if he was displeased!) We live in a different culture, where "training and instruction" is likely to be the work of both parents. That said, fathers are still held particularly responsible by God for what happens in their homes. They must not exasperate their children or provoke them to anger. We can do this in a variety of ways—favouritism, inconsistency, humiliation or ridicule. Instead, we are to both train and instruct our children in the Lord.

Instruction involves teaching them the Bible in a relevant and accessible way. Training has the idea of discipline and direction. Just as the rider steers the horse with a bit, so parents are to steer their children in the right direction. We are not to crush their personality or individuality but direct them in a loving way so that they see that disobedience and sin always have painful consequences. When we discipline our children, we follow the example of our heavenly Father (Hebrews 12:7-8).

Finally, Christians parents with young children at home are to pray regularly with them and for them. The Bible's command to pray for our church family surely includes those with whom we share a home (Ephesians 6:18; James 5:16). Without trying to be overly prescriptive, we should aim to model prayer to our children so that it seems to be as natural as breathing. It is a myth that children are always carefree. They often carry heavy burdens. We can teach them how to pray and to cast their cares on the Lord (Psalm 55:22; 1 Peter 5:7).

Cause and Effect

What happens if we fail to follow these instructions?

The hard truth is that there are always consequences for disobedience. The Bible contains several examples of weak or defective parenting. Consider Isaac's family. Of his twin sons, we're told that Isaac favoured Esau, but Rebekah favoured Jacob—and this had dire consequences for both of their sons. Jacob plotted with his mother to swindle his brother out of his father's blessing, and Esau was overcome by anger and bitterness:

> *Esau held a grudge against Jacob because of the blessing his father had given him. He said to himself, "The days of mourning for my father are near; then I will kill my brother Jacob." (Genesis 27:41)*

Later on, we read the story of Eli the priest and his sons:

> *Eli's sons were scoundrels; they had no regard for the LORD ... This sin of the young men was very great in the LORD's sight, for they were treating the LORD's offering with contempt. (1 Samuel 2:12, 17)*

Eli warned them, but he failed to discipline them, and so God pronounced judgment on Eli and his family:

> *At that time, I will carry out against Eli everything I spoke against his family—from beginning to end. For I told him that I would judge his family for ever because of the sin he knew about; his sons uttered blasphemies against God, and he failed to restrain them.*
> *(1 Samuel 3:12-13)*

Perhaps the most painful example is David and his children. David was chosen to be king over Israel because he was a man after God's own heart (13:14). The early years of his reign were marked by his faithfulness to God. But in 2 Samuel 11 he commits a horrendous sin. He takes another man's wife—Bathsheba—into his bed, and she becomes pregnant. When his initial attempts to cover his tracks fail, he has her husband killed in battle. He marries Bathsheba, and the baby is born. Does anyone suspect what has happened? Perhaps not. But the chapter ends with the ominous words:

> *But the thing David had done displeased the LORD.*
> *(2 Samuel 11:27)*

God sends the prophet Nathan to confront David:

> *Why did you despise the word of the LORD by doing what is evil in his eyes? You struck down Uriah the Hittite*

with the sword and took his wife to be your own. You killed him with the sword of the Ammonites. Now, therefore, the sword shall never depart from your house, because you despised me and took the wife of Uriah the Hittite to be your own. (12:9-10)

David confesses that he has sinned against the Lord. Nathan assures him that he has God's forgiveness—but that does not remove the word of judgment on David's family.

One son deceives and rapes his half-sister. Another son, Absalom, murders his brother in revenge. With blood on his hands, Absalom flees for his life—but comes back to try to seize the throne from his father. The cycles of deception, violence and sexual sin continue.

Serious parental failure, particularly in the example that we set to our children, can have dire consequences. David's sons did not respect their father because he had committed the same crimes as them. Although he had experienced forgiveness, he had to live with the consequences of his catastrophic moral failure. God is wonderfully gracious in his forgiveness but has never promised to remove the painful consequences of outright disobedience.

Clarity and Grace

All this needs to be said.

But it is dangerous if we take it out of context. The illustrations given above are examples of extreme moral failure leading to dire generational consequences. Does that mean that you should blame yourself and feel guilty because your children are not following the Lord?

I think we need to say three things at least.

1. CONFESS YOUR SIN

First, it is good to acknowledge that none of us have got it completely right. There is no such thing as a perfect parent. The only perfect parent is God the Father, just as God the Son is the only perfect Son. Almost every parent I speak with looks back on their experience of parenting and thinks they could have done better. We could have spent more time imaginatively teaching our children the Bible. Sometimes we said one thing and did another. Sometimes our discipline was not gentle. I remember times when, as a parent, the punishment I gave to my children did not fit the crime. Sometimes I even got the wrong criminal! And of course, we could have prayed more. There are no perfect parents.

In his grace God forgives our sins and overrules our mistakes. Many of the mistakes that we make as parents are not sinful; they're just unwise. Others are the result of our creaturely weakness and human limitations—we can't know or do everything. But sometimes we have committed what we might call parental sins. We have exasperated our children by failing to practise what we preach or allowing frustrations with life to affect the way in which we treat them. If you have acted wrongly against your children in any way, it is right to apologise and to ask for their forgiveness. But we also need to ask for God's grace. Ask God to give you a truly repentant heart.

You might want to use David's words when he confessed his disastrous sin with Bathsheba:

> *Have mercy on me, O God,*
> *according to your unfailing love;*
> *according to your great compassion*
> *blot out my transgressions.*

Wash away all my iniquity
and cleanse me from my sin. (Psalm 51:1-2)

2. REJOICE IN GOD'S FORGIVENESS

We know for certain that if we confess our sins, God is faithful to forgive our sins and to cleanse us from all unrighteousness (1 John 1:9). Having cried out for mercy after his sin with Bathsheba, David knows about the wonder of forgiveness:

Blessed is the one
whose transgressions are forgiven,
whose sins are covered.
Blessed is the one
whose sin the LORD does not count against them
and in whose spirit is no deceit. (Psalm 32:1-2)

Take these words to heart. Meditate on them. Receive them as medicine for your soul!

His mercy covers our parental sins as well as all our other sins. When we are vulnerable because of the grief caused by prodigal children, the devil will whisper in our ear that it is all our fault. All of us have made mistakes. As we look back, we may wish we had done many things differently. But when Satan points his accusing finger at us, what he says is usually a lie. If we have sought God's forgiveness, then we can put our sin behind our back just as God puts it behind his back. God does not want us to remember what he has chosen to forget. Be honest about your feelings, but don't wallow in them. Allow yourself to enjoy all God's gifts, including the gift of your children, and don't be weighed down by a burden of guilt that Christ died to remove.

3. TRUST GOD TO DO WHAT ONLY HE CAN DO

Finally, we need to recognise that even though the Bible gives us very clear guidelines on how we should bring up our children, it does not promise that if we do these things, our children will become Christians. We cannot hold God over a barrel and demand that because we have done our part, he must save our children. As we have seen, our children are born with sinful hearts. Nothing that they or we can do will free them from their sin. Our children are lost, and they need to be saved, and only God can save them.

As mentioned above, this should not lead to any form of fatalism; we have to follow God's instructions and leave the consequences to him. But we also recognise that only he can give them a new heart. No matter how godly the family is, no matter how expert the parenting, no matter how devoted or prayerful we might be, we cannot guarantee that our children will be wise in the Bible's definition of wisdom.

There is a great mystery about the way in which God chooses to save people. Without denying human responsibility, every conversion involves a miracle. And only God can work this miracle. Although we are accustomed to riding in to rescue our children when they are in trouble, in this area we are powerless. But the Lord is mighty to save—and he is not done with your family yet.

QUESTIONS

1. Feeling guilty is an occupational hazard for parents! What did you find helpful in this chapter about what we should do with those feelings?

2. Have you felt the kind of sense of failure described by Marvin and Yolanda at the start of the chapter? What are the areas that you tend to feel most guilty about?

3. Page 49 talks about 1) mistakes that were unwise rather than sinful; 2) shortcomings that are a result of our human limitations; and 3) "parental sins". As you consider your answers to question 2, which of those three categories do you think you are dealing with?

4. Spend time in prayer: repent of any sin; rejoice in Christ's forgiveness; ask God to silence the voice of false condemnation.

5. Is there anything you need to apologise to your children for? What would it look like to repent to them?

CHAPTER 4

DOES GOD PROMISE TO SAVE OUR CHILDREN?

Just Give Us Hope

Jas and Sally invited my wife and me for a meal. The room was filled with photographs celebrating their children's achievements and victories. Looking around, I suggested that they must be very proud of their kids. At this, an unexpected emotional dam began to burst.

> *Of course we are proud. But none of them are following the Lord. Sometimes we lose hope. You are a pastor. You know the Bible. Just give us hope.*

The Bible says a lot about hope. Hope is the expectation that in the end all will be well. It gives stability and security as we face the uncertainties of the future. It enables us to see light at the end of even the darkest tunnel. And hope is not just wishful thinking—for it latches on to the promises of God.

And the Bible is filled with promises which feed our hope and give us assurance for the future. Of course my friends wanted a word of hope.

Maybe that's what you're looking for too. So, does the Bible give a clear promise to Christians that their children will become believers? Is there a guarantee that we can hold onto amid the shattering pain we are feeling? And if there is no such promise, does that mean we have to abandon hope?

Holy Children?

The Bible teaches that the children of believers enjoy several privileges and blessings both in the home and in the church.

Paul describes the children of believers as being "holy". He encourages Christians to stay married to their non-Christian partners, saying…

> *For the unbelieving husband has been sanctified through his wife, and the unbelieving wife has been sanctified through her believing husband.*

He then adds…

> *Otherwise your children would be unclean, but as it is, they are holy. (1 Corinthians 7:14)*

What does Paul mean by this?

The words "sanctified" and "holy" come from the same Greek word and have the idea of being set aside. This implies that what happens to the unsaved partner and to the child is the same. However, it cannot mean that they are saved, because the Bible reminds us elsewhere that children of Christians do not become children of God until they experience the gift of new life. This gift is not based on physical parentage or parental decision. Rather…

> *to all who did receive him, to those who believed in his name, he gave the right to become children of God—children born not of natural descent, nor of human decision or a husband's will, but born of God.*
>
> *(John 1:12-13)*

Therefore, I think that what Paul is saying in 1 Corinthians 7:14 is that these children are somehow placed within a sphere of godly influence. The presence of at least one Christian parent will impact their lives in a positive way. They will be more likely to be exposed to gospel truth, which is a prerequisite for saving faith. This was what happened to Timothy, whose sincere faith in Christ had first "lived" in his grandmother Lois and in his mother Eunice (2 Timothy 1:5). There is no suggestion that their faith was somehow imparted to him. However, they created an atmosphere in which he heard the gospel and was ready to respond, even though it appears that his father was not a believer.

Children brought up in a Christian home will enjoy the privilege of Bible teaching and godly examples in the home and the church. But such privilege does not amount to the gift of salvation. As we have seen, that gift is not within our power.

But it is within God's. So is there somewhere else in the Bible where God promises the gift of salvation to our children?

In my experience, people turn to two or three places to bolster the idea that God guarantees that our children will become Christians.

Train up a Child

The most commonly quoted Bible verse on this subject is probably Proverbs 22:6:

> *Train up a child in the way he should go;*
> *even when he is old he will not depart from it. (ESV)*

There seems to be a case of cause-and-effect in this verse: if parents train their children and point them in the right direction, then they will never turn from it. Some people understand this verse to mean that—while the effects may take time and faith may lie dormant for years—in the end, if we get it right, our children will become Christians.

But there are a number of problems with this argument.

For one thing, in the context of the book of Proverbs, this verse is not talking about salvation but about a child following the moral direction and instruction of their parents.

In addition, the book of Proverbs is a wisdom book which gives us rules of thumb rather than binding promises. Generally speaking, the wise conduct it recommends will lead to positive results: the conscientious person will prosper, and the lazy person will not; the person who keeps good company will succeed, and the person who keeps bad company will fail; wise people do well, and foolish people don't. But this is not always the case. Alongside the book of Proverbs, we have the books of Job and Ecclesiastes, and several psalms, which show that often the wicked prosper and the godly suffer.

Finally, such a reading of this verse places our confidence in our own parenting skills rather than the grace of God. As we have already seen, none of us can claim to be perfect parents. How often have we failed to bring up our children in the way in which they should go? We have to put our hope in God's grace and not in our own achievements.

We may take this verse as a general principle but not as a cast-iron guarantee. We cannot hold God to a promise that he has not made.

You and Your Household

Another place that people turn to is the Acts of the Apostles. Let me give two examples. At the end of his sermon on the day of Pentecost, Peter offers the gift of salvation to all who will repent and be baptised in the name of Jesus. He concludes:

> *The promise is for you and your children and for all who are far off—for all whom the Lord our God will call.*
>
> *(Acts 2:39)*

Peter is speaking to Jews gathered in Jerusalem from across the diaspora. But the message is not just for Jewish people. The gift of many languages given on the day of Pentecost is an indication that the gospel promise crosses all cultural, social and geographical boundaries. Nor is it confined to one generation. It applies to them and their children. Everyone who accepts the message, repents of their sin and turns to Christ will be saved.

It's certainly wonderful news—but notice that this is not an unconditional promise of forgiveness to our offspring. The promise depends on the proper response of repentance and faith. Just as those Gentiles who are far off are not automatically saved, so our children must also exercise faith to experience God's grace.

Another verse which is commonly quoted is Acts 16:31. In response to the Philippian jailer's question—"What must I do to be saved?"—Paul answers:

> *Believe in the Lord Jesus, and you will be saved—you and your household. (v 31)*

Once again, the promise is comprehensive. Any person within the household of the jailer who has faith will experience salvation. But like Peter's words on the day of Pentecost, the offer is conditional. Only those who exercise faith will experience the benefits of salvation.

Many Christians are convinced that it is right to baptise the children of Christian parents and that in doing so, we bring those infants into the covenant community (that is, the people of God). There are a wide range of opinions on the significance of this. Perhaps the child is included for a while, so that a small child who passes away is "covered" by their parents. But even those who believe infants should be baptised also recognise that these same children will eventually need to exercise personal faith in order to be saved. The Bible does not teach that the act of baptism imparts salvation to the child.

"Once Saved, Always Saved"

Another idea that parents often hold onto is that we cannot lose our salvation. This is often expressed with the phrase "once saved, always saved". If our child professed faith when they were younger, is this sufficient grounds for hope?

Let me say three things.

First, the Bible does teach that someone who has genuinely become a Christian will never lose their salvation. No one can snatch us from God's hand (John 10:27-30) or separate us from his love (Romans 8:31-39). The moment we believe, we are sealed with the Holy Spirit, who guarantees our future inheritance (Ephesians 1:13-14). The God who has begun a good work in us will bring it to completion (Philippians 1:6). Whatever we have to pass through in this life, God will guard us and bring us safely home (1 Peter 1:3-5). We are completely secure in our salvation.

Second, the Bible also teaches that there is such a thing as a "false believer". This is the person who claims to believe and yet shows no evidence of a transformed life. Jesus warned that we need to recognise the genuineness of faith by the fruit that it produces (Matthew 7:16-20). Not everyone who claims to have faith is really saved, and not everyone who says, "Lord, Lord" will enter the kingdom of heaven (v 21-23).

The phrase "once saved, always saved" can therefore be misleading. If the person was genuinely saved with the evidence of a changed life, then it is true. But if there is no fruit in their lives, then that is evidence that they were not saved in the first place. I think of the father who says to me:

> *My son gave his heart to Jesus when he was six. He always enjoyed family worship. He was baptised when he was 16. He may not be walking with the Lord at the moment, but I know he is saved because he trusted Jesus, and that's all that matters.*

He's right that we're saved by faith alone—but saving faith is always accompanied by the evidence of a changed life. It is those who persevere to the end who are saved (Matthew 10:22).

Third, we do not know the heart. When children are small, it's normal for them to echo the faith of their parents. This is not necessarily an indication of saving faith. It might be. But it might not be. If they are not currently "walking with the Lord", it might be because their faith was not genuine in the first place. Or it might be that they are in a backslidden condition. We just don't know. And because we don't know, it is not enough to rest our hope on a mere profession of faith at any age.

Many People in This City

So, if the Bible does not guarantee that our children will be saved, does this mean that we are left in despair? Are there any grounds for legitimate hope?

I think there are.

God has been abundantly gracious to our children by placing them in an environment of godly influence. As we have seen, this is an amazing privilege. We cannot assume that they will be saved, but we can pray with real faith and confidence that the Lord has good purposes for them.

When Paul was in the midst of a difficult period of ministry in Corinth, the Lord brought him a word of assurance in a vision:

> *Do not be afraid; keep on speaking, do not be silent. For I am with you, and no one is going to attack and harm you, because I have many people in this city.*
>
> *(Acts 18:9-10)*

These promises encouraged Paul to persevere. We cannot rip them out of context and apply them in an illegitimate way. But these verses do assure us of God's presence with us whenever we seek to serve him. They also encourage us to believe he is able to protect us from danger. This is not an absolute promise for all time, because we know that later Paul would experience both attacks and imprisonment. But God assures him that he will be safe until his work in Corinth is accomplished. But it is the last part of the promise that is particularly pertinent to us here. God will protect Paul because…

I have many people in this city.

God knows who he will save and how he will save them. Corinth had a reputation for being a desperately wicked city, but this could not defeat God's grace. Paul was to persevere, knowing that God could do what he (Paul) could not.

And the same applies with our children. We cannot give them the gift of salvation, but God can. No heart is so closed and deadened to the gospel that God cannot breathe new life into it. This should ignite hope within our hearts. And God wants us to be a people of hope. God has placed our children in a family where they have heard the good news of the gospel and can continue to hear it. This should bring us great encouragement.

No One Is Too Difficult

Sometimes God answers our prayers in unexpected ways.

On 27th December 2004, my wife and I had a phone call from friends to tell us that their son Tony had gone missing after the terrible Boxing Day tsunami which had struck the day before. We had known Tony as a little boy when his family were part of the church in which we worshipped. As a young man, he had rejected his parents' faith and adopted a lifestyle which caused them immense pain. He was in Thailand when the tsunami hit.

A few days later we heard that he was safe.

A few months later we heard his remarkable story.

Caught in a room almost fully submerged under water, he cried out to God for mercy. He survived and returned to the UK, but he didn't become a Christian. Then he was involved in a serious motorcycle accident. Lying in a hospital bed, he realised that he was on the point of wasting the second chance that God had given him to believe. This time he cried out to God for salvation. And it was real. Tony began to serve God on board one of the Operation Mobilisation missionary ships. God gave him a wife and a family, and he rejoices today in the amazing grace of God.

Not many conversions are as dramatic as this one, but every conversion is supernatural. During my ministry I have heard numerous stories of rebellious children who have come to faith. I think of one man in his 40s who had rejected his parents' faith since his early teens, but who was converted at his dad's funeral.

God can save anyone, at any time and in any way. Don't give up! Pray in hope.

People of Hope

We are to be people whose hope is in God alone.

The Bible is clear:

His pleasure is not in the strength of the horse,
nor his delight in the legs of the warrior;

the Lord delights in those who fear him,
who put their hope in his unfailing love.
(Psalm 147:10-11)

The people of Israel were always tempted to look to human armies to give them victory in battle.

But God does not need military strength to bring about his purposes. What does God look for in us when we come before him in all our need? The person he delights in is the one who fears him and bases all their hopes and expectations on his "unfailing love".

This is a translation of the Hebrew word *hesed*, which I think is one of the most beautiful words in the whole Bible. When my wife and I retired to Birmingham, we decided to name our house "Hesed". My daughter bought us a plaque which now hangs in the entrance hall. It says that this word…

… is wrapping up in itself all the positive attributes of God: love, covenant faithfulness, mercy, grace, kindness, loyalty—in short, acts of devotion and loving kindness that go beyond the requirements of duty.

This gets to the heart of who God is. He is full of *hesed*—unfailing love. Knowing this is an immense encouragement to persevere in loving and praying for our children with the eager and genuine hope that God will one day save them. Such hope is not based on a particular promise in the Bible but flows from everything we know about God's character.

Coming to God with a sense of great need delights him. I may not be able to do great and impressive things for God, but I can cast myself upon him in desperation and cling to him in hope. And amazingly, this is the very thing that delights his heart.

Hope gives fuel to prayer. But what should we pray? This will be the theme of the next chapter.

QUESTIONS

1. Before reading this chapter, how hopeful were you for your unsaved children? What was that hope (or lack of it) based on? What about now?
2. What privileges, short of saving faith, do children brought up in Christian homes enjoy?
3. How can we keep our hope alive when our children seem to be hardened towards the gospel?
4. Read the definition of God's unfailing *hesed* love again. How does this help us to keep on loving children who do not love Jesus?

CHAPTER 5

WHAT SHOULD WE PRAY?

The Best Thing You Can Do

As I prepared to write this chapter, my wife and I received a WhatsApp message from our fellowship group. It was from a young couple excitedly reporting that, after an eventful night, they were currently in the delivery suite awaiting the birth of their first child.

Our immediate reaction was to pray for a safe delivery—and for the salvation of the little one.

The best thing we can ever do for a child is to pray for them.

And yet most of us struggle with prayer. I have yet to meet the person who says that prayer is easy. Most of us are dissatisfied with our prayer lives. What is wrong with me? My theology tells me that prayer is vital. My Bible encourages me to pray without ceasing. My needs are so great that only my heavenly Father is sufficient to meet them. And yet I feel as if I fail in this area again and again.

And that gives rise to all sorts of fears. *Maybe my children didn't become Christians because I didn't pray enough. Maybe my prayers were not sufficient or I prayed for the wrong things. Perhaps I just didn't have enough faith.*

It is amazing how many thoughts like these flood into our minds when we try to pray. We are swamped with a sense of guilt or confusion. We know we should do better, but a healthy prayer life feels just beyond our grasp.

Casting Ourselves on God

Can I suggest that these negative thoughts betray a misunderstanding of the nature of prayer? We know that we're saved by grace alone through faith alone, and yet when we pray, this theology goes right out of the window. Instead, we think we need to earn a hearing from God by the length or passion or eloquence of our petitions.

But true prayer is coming to God without pretence as a little child. Jesus encourages us to come just as we are:

> *Come to me, all you who are weary and burdened, and I will give you rest. (Matthew 11:28)*

The only condition for coming is a sense of weariness and need and a desire to be free from the burden which is weighing us down. If your greatest burden is the fact that your children are not saved, then this verse is for you! Don't try to wrap up your prayers in eloquent language. Come as you are, ready to place your children into God's hands.

When we look at Jesus' teaching about prayer, what is most remarkable is his emphasis on the distance that exists between the pray-er and the one they are approaching.

For example, he tells a story about a powerless widow and a powerful judge (Luke 18:1-8). Jesus wants to encourage us to persevere in prayer—the widow just won't give up. She keeps coming to the judge, pleading for justice against an adversary—and eventually the judge gives in, simply to get her off his case. Jesus' point is: how much more confident can we then be that the perfect God of justice will answer our pleas? So pray and keep praying, each and every day.

But Jesus is also teaching that we can bring our needs before God in desperation. Prayer is not a negotiation between equals—it is a declaration of our absolute dependence on God. We don't need to be embarrassed about how needy we feel.

All Your Anxiety...

There is a great example of this kind of prayer in the story of King Hezekiah. He was one of the few good kings in the Old Testament. During his reign, the city of Jerusalem was surrounded by the seemingly invincible armies of Assyria. When their threats reached Hezekiah, "he tore his clothes and put on sackcloth and went into the temple of the LORD" (2 Kings 19:1). He sent a message to the prophet Isaiah, asking him to pray.

Soon after, Hezekiah received a letter from the commander of the Assyrian army, which mocked his confidence in God. How did he respond?

> *Hezekiah received the letter from the messengers and read it. Then he went up to the temple of the LORD and spread it out before the LORD. (v 14)*

What a wonderful picture of prayer! By laying the letter before God, Hezekiah was confessing that the situation was too big for him. He did not have the resources to meet this threat. He could not carry this burden. So instead, he placed it before God and handed it over to him.

At the conclusion of the chapter we read:

> *That night the angel of the LORD went out and put to death a hundred and eighty-five thousand in the Assyrian camp. When the people got up the next morning—there were all the dead bodies! So Sennacherib king of Assyria broke camp and withdrew. He returned to Nineveh and stayed there. (v 35-36)*

Hezekiah prayed—and the Lord rescued Jerusalem. Isn't this what we have to do with our children? We cannot give them the gift of life. It is beyond us. But God can do it. Like Hezekiah, we can lay our children before God.

Perhaps you feel as though you're already doing that. We saw earlier that the story of the persistent widow teaches us to persevere in prayer. If you are praying for unsaved children, you will probably pray for them every day—perhaps even more than once a day. That's a good thing.

For some of us, though, the problem is that after we have laid the burden at God's feet, we try to pick it up again. We revert to worrying about our children instead of placing them in God's hands and leaving them with him. Genuine prayerful concern is replaced by energy-sapping anxiety.

There is an old hymn which asks the question:

> *Is there a heart o'erbound by sorrow?*
> *Is there a life weighed down by care?*[4]

It then gives a prescription:

Come to the cross, each burden bearing;
All your anxiety—leave it there.

This is reinforced in the refrain:

All your anxiety, all your care,
Bring to the mercy seat, leave it there,
Never a burden he cannot bear,
Never a friend like Jesus!

Bringing the burden to God is comparatively easy. The real challenge is leaving it there! You have prayed, and the situation doesn't seem to have changed. Your children are just as hard as ever. It takes determination, perseverance and grit to keep bringing them to the Lord—and then to leave them in God's good keeping for another day.

Edward H. Joy, the author of the hymn, was inspired by Peter's words:

Humble yourselves, therefore, under God's mighty hand, that he may lift you up in due time. Cast all your anxiety on him because he cares for you. (1 Peter 5:6-7)

Peter encourages you to cast your anxieties on God. You can do so because you know that he cares for you. And because he cares for your children—more than you ever can. So when you pray, you are running with the grain of God's character. But notice the warning about humility. It is often our pride that makes us think that, having cast our burdens upon God, we have to help him to carry them for us! Like Hezekiah, God wants you to lay at his feet those concerns which weigh down your heart.

Whom Does God Delight In?

In the last chapter, we quoted from Psalm 147:

> *The Lord delights in those who fear him,*
> *who put their hope in his unfailing love. (v 11)*

Earlier in the psalm, there are two verses that stand side by side and which have always been an encouragement in my prayer life.

In verse 4, the psalmist reflects on the greatness of God:

> *He determines the number of the stars*
> *and calls them each by name.*

Like a shepherd who knows his flock, God knows every one of the stars in the universe. Bearing in mind that in the Milky Way alone there are an estimated 100 billion stars and that the Milky Way is one of 100 billion galaxies, this is a stunning statement!

It is tempting to imagine that a God who is engaged in running a universe as vast as ours would have no time for our needs. But the verse before that one states:

> *He heals the broken-hearted*
> *and binds up their wounds. (v 3)*

When you stumble into your Father's presence with a heart that is broken and wounds which seem unbearable, he doesn't ignore you because his mind is elsewhere controlling the spinning galaxies. He draws you near in a close embrace and heals your broken heart and attends to your painful wounds. Of course, these assurances help us in whatever area we are praying. But I think they have a particular relevance when we come before God weighed down with the burden of unsaved children.

Imagine a symphony orchestra in the middle of a prestigious performance. With great skill the conductor leads the musicians in a glorious celebration of a magnificent piece of music. Suddenly his little four-year-old son stumbles onto the platform. He has skinned his knee, and only daddy can bring the comfort he needs. Without ceasing to lead the orchestra, the conductor gathers up his son and kisses away the tears. In the same way, our God conducts the symphony of the stars and at the same time welcomes each of his children as if they were the only one longing for his attention. Some come overflowing with joy; others stumble into his presence broken with grief. Some approach full of fear or doubt, while others come overwhelmed with a sense of guilt and shame. But an infinite God receives each one and meets their needs out of his infinite resources.

God is never too busy or preoccupied to receive you when you bring your burdens into his presence. God cares for your children. That is such an encouragement when we are struggling to persevere in prayer.

What Should We Pray For?

It's hard to know what to pray sometimes; or we've been praying for so many years that we've run out of steam and lost momentum. So, to reinvigorate your prayers for your children, here are ten ways you can pray. They've been drawn from conversations I've had with parents in pain who have shared some of the substance of their prayers. Each situation has its own complications, but over time several common themes have emerged.

1. *Pray for their conversion.* This is the obvious place to begin. As we have seen, every conversion is a miracle. God needs to take away the heart of stone and in its place put a heart of flesh (Ezekiel 36:26-27). At this point it is quite easy to become knotted up by our theology. What if God has not chosen them? Where does human responsibility begin? What is the place of prayer? Without being overly simplistic, my advice is to simply set these matters aside and cling to the fact that God encourages us to pray for lost people to be saved. We can pray in the face of mystery without full comprehension. So come with childlike faith and ask for the one thing above everything else that you long for. You can leave the results with God. Pray that God will deliver your child from the dominion of darkness and transfer them to the kingdom of his Son (Colossians 1:13).

2. *Pray for exposures to the faith.* One parent said to me, "I'm praying that my daughter will come into contact with the gospel at work—I know that there are at least two Christians in the school where she teaches". The contact might come through conversations, social media, music or some other means. It is amazing how often God uses unexpected and unforeseen methods to awaken dull consciences. So be imaginative! Pray for providential encounters.

3. *Pray that God would break into your child's life, however much it costs.* We want our children to be happy, and most parents will do anything in their power to protect their children from disappointment and difficulty. But

their eternal salvation is more important than any temporary happiness in this world. When they go through hard times, we rightly do whatever we can to support them, but we can also pray that God will use the situation to open their eyes.

4. *Pray that they may remember things that they learned while they were growing up.* Children brought up in a Christian home will be exposed to so much biblical truth during their formative years. Many of these great truths are never truly forgotten. Pray that the Holy Spirit would bring back to mind the seeds that were planted in their hearts. Ask God to awaken within them a yearning for himself (Psalm 42:1).

5. *Pray that the devil would not blind their eyes to the truth.* We are engaged in a spiritual battle (Ephesians 6:10-20). I remember seeing a Christian poster many years ago. The light of the moon streams through a window and illuminates a small child lying in bed. On his knees next to the bed we see a man, presumably this child's father, deep in passionate prayer. Underneath are the words "Spiritual Warfare". Pray that the devil will not snatch away the seed of God's word (Matthew 13:4, 18-19). Ask God to protect them from the snares of the evil one (2 Timothy 2:22-26).

6. *Pray for all aspects of their lives.* Pray for their marriages. Pray for their children. Pray about their work stresses and house moves. Pray about their small needs and big decisions. And then don't be embarrassed to tell them how you've been praying—it may give them pause for thought when they see God answer. (And

if you have children who are walking with the Lord, don't neglect to pray for them too. I have met parents whose children turned away from the faith in their 20s or 30s. Avoid complacency.)

7. *Pray for the influence of other Christians in their lives.* We sometimes think that they can only be saved through our witness. But the Lord might choose to use someone else to lead them to Christ. Pray for Christians that they might meet at university or in the workplace. I witnessed to my sister for many years, but it was my son who led her to Christ. Ask God to give them gracious and tenacious Christian friends. Pray that any encounter with believers or with church may be positive. Pray that the Christians they meet would be full of grace.

8. *Pray for the influence of their own children.* If you have grandchildren, pray that they might become Christians but also that they may influence their parents. I have seen this happening in a number of ways. When faced with the challenge of bringing up their own kids, folks will often remember the wonderful influence of a Christian home or the excitement of a Christian camp when they were young. They want their own children to share this experience. So pray that your grandchildren may point them to the Lord. In several cases I have seen this as the first step back to church and then into Christ.

9. *Pray for yourself.* Ask for God's help to be faithful, wise and loving. Pray that you would grow through the pain that you are experiencing. Pray that you don't

become bitter or resentful towards God. Pray that you will be able to persevere and not give up.

10. *Pray for other parents with unsaved children.* Consider doing this together. In one of the churches I served, there was a regular prayer meeting for "Parents in Pain". There is a wonderful fellowship when we share our common burdens. And for many of us, praying with and for other people often seems easier than praying on our own.

There is so much more that I could say. Pray for your children passionately and relentlessly. Persevere (1 Thessalonians 5:17). Look to God and not to other people. If your spouse is a believer, pray together as husband and wife. Be honest with God and tell him how you feel. And above everything, be patient. We walk by faith and not by sight (2 Corinthians 5:7). Although we can't manipulate God or force his hand, we can remind him of his promises.

> *Let us not become weary in doing good, for at the proper time we will reap a harvest if we do not give up.*
> *(Galatians 6:9)*

God's timing is not the same as ours. Sometimes he opens his hand one finger at a time! We are creatures of a moment whereas he is the God of eternity. You cannot hold an hourglass to the creator of time. God loves your children more than you ever will, so by prayer place them into his hands and learn to leave them there.

QUESTIONS

1. "My theology tells me that prayer is vital. My Bible encourages me to pray without ceasing. My needs are so great that only my heavenly Father is sufficient to meet them. And I feel as if I fail here again and again" (p 67). Have you felt a similar gap between your belief and practice? Why do you think that is?

2. Look at the parable of the persistent widow in Luke 18:1-8. How does this encourage you in your prayers for your prodigal children?

3. Prayer involves spiritual warfare. How does this affect our approach to prayer? How does it affect the things we pray for?

4. Look through the list of ten prayer suggestions given above. What other things might you pray for unsaved children? Why not put down this book and begin right now?

CHAPTER 6

HOW DO WE SHOW LOVE TO OUR UNSAVED CHILDREN?

What Does God Expect?

Graham and Pauline had two sons.

Nick, the oldest, lived a couple of streets away. He visited his mum and dad at least once a week. Nothing was too much trouble. His wife, Mary, stopped by every other day, and Graham and Pauline saw enough, but not too much, of their grandchildren. Nick was happy for the kids to come to church, and he and Mary would attend family services on special occasions. But he had never made a profession of faith.

Daniel, their younger son, had professed faith and been baptised as a teenager. But when he went to university, it all went wrong. He dropped out before the end of his first year and got into debt because of a gambling addiction. Since then, he had been through a whole series of disastrous relationships. He never visited his parents except when he needed money. It always ended in a row.

Graham confided in me:

> *We love both our kids. They both need the Lord. But it's easy to love Nick. Loving Daniel is really hard work!*

As we have seen, there is a wide spectrum of experiences when it comes to prodigal children. But whether your child is more like Nick or more like Daniel, the question remains the same—how do we treat children who don't love Jesus?

In one sense, the answer is pretty straightforward. We have to love our children lavishly, whether or not they become Christians. We need to remind them constantly that they are always our children and to assure them that we will never walk away from them. The prodigal son broke his father's heart, but he could not destroy his father's love. If we are Christians, we have experienced God's grace—a love which is undeserved, unmerited and unwarranted. It is lavish, sacrificial and tenacious. We are to be characterised by the same kind of love.

We have already looked at Hosea 11, where God compares his love to the yearning compassion of a father. The prophet Isaiah uses the image of a mother's love to describe the unyielding love of God. Israel feel that God has forgotten and forsaken them. In response God says:

> *Can a mother forget the baby at her breast*
> *and have no compassion on the child she has borne?*
> *Though she may forget,*
> *I will not forget you!*

See, I have engraved you on the palms of my hands;
your walls are ever before me. (Isaiah 49:15-16)

It is almost impossible to imagine that a mother would have no compassion for the child that she has carried for nine months. But God's love is greater still. Even when the people of Israel have rejected God and turned their backs on him, he has not rejected them. He still loves them and pursues them with purposes of grace. As we read later:

"Though the mountains be shaken
and the hills be removed,
yet my unfailing love for you will not be shaken
nor my covenant of peace be removed,"
says the LORD, who has compassion on you. (54:11)

The theme of both Hosea and Isaiah is the invincibility of God's love. But the fact that they use parental illustrations suggests that this is the way in which God wants parents to behave.

So we are to love our children whether they are saved or not. But this raises several other questions. We will spend the rest of this chapter trying to answer these questions.

What Does This Love Look Like?

God's love is the gold standard by which we are to measure our own.

In Exodus 33 Moses asks God to show him his glory. In response the Lord appears to Moses with this proclamation:

The LORD, the LORD, the compassionate and gracious God, slow to anger, abounding in love and faithfulness, maintaining love to thousands, and forgiving wickedness, rebellion and sin. Yet he does not leave the guilty unpunished; he punishes the children and their children for the sin of the parents to the third and fourth generation. (Exodus 34:6-7)

God's love is his glory. Look at the words that he uses. His love is "compassionate" and tender-hearted. It is "gracious"—moving out towards undeserving people in order to bestow free and full forgiveness. It is "slow to anger" or long-suffering, not treating us as our sins deserve. The final word "love" is a translation of that Hebrew word *hesed*. This is God's persistent and unconditional tenderness, kindness and mercy, expressed in his selfless concern for our welfare.

God's love leads to forgiveness for rebels. But it does not leave the guilty unpunished. This raises the question: how can God forgive sin without compromising his justice? The answer, of course, is that this is only possible through the death of Christ, which is not only the supreme demonstration of God's love but also the vindication of his uncompromising justice.

You see, at just the right time, when we were still powerless, Christ died for the ungodly. Very rarely will anyone die for a righteous person, though for a good person someone might possibly dare to die. But God demonstrates his own love for us in this: while we were still sinners, Christ died for us. (Romans 5:6-8)

God's love in Christ is undeserved, extravagant and immensely costly. Does our love ever approach anything like this?

Paul helps us to ground this in our experience by giving us a description of love in 1 Corinthians 13:

Love is patient, love is kind. It does not envy, it does not boast, it is not proud. It does not dishonour others, it is not self-seeking, it is not easily angered, it keeps no record of wrongs. Love does not delight in evil but rejoices with the truth. It always protects, always trusts, always hopes, always perseveres.

Love never fails. (v 4-8a)

Our love for our children is supposed to resemble this! It will express itself in different ways in different contexts. But consider for a moment how Paul's description maps onto your relationship with your unsaved child:

- *Love is patient.* Do I show my irritation when their lateness or messiness or something else annoys me? Does my frustration make me impatient?
- *Love is kind.* Am I generous with my time and attention? Am I interested in the things that they're interested in? Am I really engaged in their lives?
- *It does not envy.* Does the fact that I envy other parents whose children are walking with the Lord cause me to be resentful and angry with my own children?
- *It does not boast, it is not proud.* Do I boast about their siblings who are doing well and thereby make them feel unloved or unappreciated? Do they sense that I love my Christian children more than I love them?
- *It does not dishonour others.* Do I treat them with respect? Would I be happy for them to overhear the conversations I have about them with my friends?

- *It is not self-seeking.* Am I more concerned about my own reputation and what people might think about me than I am with trying to win their hearts for Jesus?
- *It is not easily angered.* Does my anguish turn to anger and make me snappy and critical? Do I use sharp and unkind words when I speak with them?
- *It keeps no record of wrongs.* Am I always bringing up that thing that happened ages ago? Am I quick to forgive?
- *Love does not delight in evil but rejoices with the truth.* Do I love them enough to be honest with them about what the Bible teaches even when they don't want to listen? Can I do this gently and graciously?
- *It always protects.* Do I do everything I can to support them (even though I may not be able to rescue them from the consequences of their actions)?
- *Always trusts and always hopes.* Is my love for them fuelled by my trust in God, or do I let despair and hopelessness affect the way in which I treat them?
- *Always perseveres.* Do I continue to tell my children that I love them or do I leave them to guess? Do they know that they do not need to earn my love? Do I affirm them even when I don't affirm their lifestyle?
- *Love never fails.* Am I patient when they continue in unbelief for years?

Pause to take in that list again. In what ways is the Spirit prompting you to repent and seek his help to change?

Where Does My Highest Allegiance Lie?

I have often heard parents say that they love their children unconditionally. But is this right? Yes, we are to love our children sacrificially—but we must never forget that we have a higher allegiance.

Early in his ministry, Jesus was confronted with the unbelief of his own family. His claims seemed to them to be preposterous, and they thought that he was "out of his mind"—so they set out to take charge of him (Mark 3:20-21). This was an opportunity for Jesus to teach that spiritual ties are stronger than ties of blood:

> *A crowd was sitting round him, and they told him, "Your mother and brothers are outside looking for you."*
>
> *"Who are my mother and my brothers?" he asked.*
>
> *Then he looked at those seated in a circle round him and said, "Here are my mother and my brothers! Whoever does God's will is my brother and sister and mother."*
>
> *(v 32-35)*

Jesus is not throwing off all family ties—later he shows a son's devotion to his mother when he makes provision for Mary at the cross (John 19:25-27). Honouring family responsibilities is important:

> *Anyone who does not provide for their relatives, and especially for their own household, has denied the faith and is worse than an unbeliever. (1 Timothy 5:8)*

We belong to a natural family, and we owe them a debt of love and care and commitment. But if we're a Christian, we also belong to a spiritual family—and they have a claim to our loyalty and love as well. My children need to understand that I have responsibilities to my spiritual family just as my spiritual family needs to understand that I have responsibilities to my children.

This will impact the amount of time I can give to my children. I cannot always be relied upon to babysit my grandchildren, for instance, or to drop everything to fit around my son's or daughter's busy lifestyle. On the other hand, I need to be careful that I am not so absorbed in church activities that my own children feel neglected or unloved.

But my ultimate allegiance is to Christ. Just before Jesus sends his disciples out on their first missionary journey, he gives them some striking instructions:

> *Do not suppose that I have come to bring peace to the earth. I did not come to bring peace, but a sword. For I have come to turn*
>
> *"a man against his father,*
> *a daughter against her mother,*
> *a daughter-in-law against her mother-in-law—*
> *a man's enemies will be the members of his own household." (Matthew 10:34-36)*

The gospel causes divisions which can even cut across family relationships. Sometimes it leaves us with a painful choice. Them or him?

Jesus goes on:

> *Anyone who loves their father or mother more than me is not worthy of me; anyone who loves their son or daughter more than me is not worthy of me. Whoever does not*

> *take up their cross and follow me is not worthy of me. Whoever finds their life will lose it, and whoever loses their life for my sake will find it. (v 37-39)*

These words are intended to be shocking! Jesus wants us to recognise that our highest allegiance and commitment must be to him. Following Jesus requires that we abandon the absolute loyalty and commitment that we might have to anyone or anything else. Jesus uses hyperbole—over-the-top language—to make his point. He is not telling us to hate our children but rather that we should love him more than we love them. We should do everything that we can to avoid alienation from our children, but sometimes those we love will not understand our devotion to Christ, and that will create a distance between us. In some cultures, this distance is real and obvious—converts to Christ are cut off by their family, or worse. In the majority culture in the West, this relational distance is probably much more subtle.

This may be hard to hear. We love our kids, and we have a history with them. They are a powerful and present reality in our lives. God, on the other hand, is invisible—we may not always feel the immediacy and intensity of emotion towards him that we feel towards our children. But Christ is unequivocal in his challenge to put him first in all that we believe and do.

For example, loving Christ will mean that we give allegiance to the truths that he teaches. Does the experience of having an unbelieving child tempt me to water down my beliefs? Is it true that Jesus is the only way to God? Would God really send *good people* (like my son) to hell? Is the Bible as clear as I thought it was about same-sex relationships when my daughter and her partner seem to be so happy?

Faithfulness to Christ will mean that we will resist these temptations and pursue whole-hearted devotion to Jesus—even if, despite our best efforts, this creates a distance with our biological family.

How Can I Love Them While Protecting My Marriage and My Family?

Our non-Christian children can sometimes put a strain on our marriage or our relationships with other members of the family. This is particularly true if they struggle with life-changing addictions or mental-health challenges. Even if they don't, there can be a sense of cultural dissonance in a family between those who are Christians and those who are not. This can develop into a kind of "us and them" situation.

There are a few principles to remember in this area. First, if we are married, God's blueprint is that marriage becomes our primary relationship:

> *A man leaves his father and mother and is united to his wife, and they become one flesh.*
>
> *(Genesis 2:24, quoted in Matthew 19:5 and Ephesians 5:31)*

Husbands are to love and honour their wives more than they honour their parents and more than they honour their children. My commitment to my wife takes precedence over my commitment to my children.

This means that we must not let our unsaved children drive a wedge between us and our spouse. Disappointment can put pressure on a marriage. Anger with the situation may be redirected into irritation or even bitterness towards our partner. The concern for our child becomes a barrier between us rather than deepening our dependence on God and mutual support.

It may be particularly difficult if you're married to a non-Christian. How lonely it can be when your spouse does not share your concerns. They may even feel a sense of vindication that your child favours their unbelief rather than your faith in Christ. It's easy for this to lead to an even greater sense of failure, recrimination and guilt. If that's you, you are not alone. Everything we thought about in chapter 3 is just as abundantly true for you as it is for your friends who are married to believers.

We also need to be alert to the way in which one child's unbelief might affect their siblings. Families are vulnerable when under pressure. The other children may then feel sidelined or neglected. We need to set boundaries and refuse to accept destructive behaviour. If we have children still living at home, on occasions it may be necessary to ask a rebellious young adult to leave. We may need to seek professional support from outside the home.

A slightly different case is when the child is not outwardly wayward but is vocal in their rejection of the gospel in a way that is negatively influencing younger siblings. Being loving towards a child does not mean allowing them to say what they like when under your roof. You need to set clear boundaries in order to protect your other children.

How Can I Love When the Going Gets Tough?

It's hard to love like this. We may share many good moments with our children, but their hearts don't seem to change. Of course, we go on loving them. As we have seen, there's a gravity about love, and you don't argue with gravity. But the kind of love that we have described in this chapter is supernatural.

You can't do this with your own resources. But the great thing is that you don't have to! You can draw on God's grace to help you to persevere in faith and hope and love.

Over the years I have discovered that the way to grow in my love for God and for others is to dwell often and long on his love for me.

This is exactly what Paul does in the great prayer recorded in Ephesians 3:17-19:

> *I pray that you, being rooted and established in love, may have power, together with all the Lord's holy people, to grasp how wide and long and high and deep is the love of Christ, and to know this love that surpasses knowledge—that you may be filled to the measure of all the fullness of God.*

Paul's prayer can be summarised in just one short sentence: God loves you more than you can imagine, and he wants you to know it. Knowing that we are loved will give us the stability of a tree with its roots sunk deeply into the refreshing soil or of a building established on solid foundations (v 17). Life may be tough, but we can joyfully endure when we know that we are loved by God.

In order to describe this love, Paul uses a number of dimensional adjectives—it is wide and long and high and deep.

It is so wide that it crosses all barriers and then encompasses all types of people—even my wayward son or daughter! As to length, it is eternal. I have loved my children for as long as they have lived, but God's love stretches back into eternity before the first flicker of light. And it is so high that it can raise rebels to sit with Christ in the heavenly realms, transporting them from "the guttermost to the uttermost". But the most remarkable thing about this love is its depths. It is as deep as Calvary. It took Christ from the throne of heaven to a wooden stake on a bleak hillside outside Jerusalem.

This love surpasses knowledge. As we reflect upon it, we find that it kindles a flame of love in our own hearts. We will never be able to love our children as much as God does. But as we bask in his love, we will begin to love in a way that resembles his love. God knows the worst about us, and yet he still loves us. So even when your child is breaking your heart, ask God to give you this kind of love for them. In loving our children this way we are in some way emulating the love of God.

QUESTIONS

1. Which of the biblical descriptions of God's love in this chapter most struck you? What would it look like if parents loved their children in this way?
2. Look at the list of questions based on the description of love in 1 Corinthians 13. In which of these areas do you find it most difficult to be loving?
3. In your relationship with your children, have you ever been tempted to put them above Jesus, or to change your theology or compromise your faith? How so?
4. How might you need to guard your marriage and your family in your situation?
5. Why do we doubt God's love? Read Romans 8:31-39. How does Paul help us to understand God's love in these verses?

CHAPTER 7

AM I STILL ALLOWED TO LOVE HIM?

How Could I Have Got It So Wrong?

She stood at the end of a long queue, waiting to talk with me. I had just spoken at a large Christian conference on what the Bible teaches about sexuality. In my talk I had tried to be both biblically faithful and pastorally sensitive. I wanted to speak honestly and yet compassionately.

After the session, lots of people wanted to engage and I must have been fielding questions for almost an hour when this lady finally got to speak to me.

She looked nervous and embarrassed. With a faltering voice she managed to get out the question that had been troubling her:

> *My son just had his 20th birthday. He's in his second year at university. He came home at Easter, and me and his dad knew that something was wrong. After three days he plucked up courage to tell us that he was gay*

and that he had just started a relationship with someone at his college. I'm a Christian, and I believe the Bible. I thought my son was also a Christian, but now he tells us that he wants nothing to do with the Christian faith anymore and that he just wants to be himself. I agree with everything you said today. But here's my question: if my son is gay, am I still allowed to love him?

Her words stopped me in my tracks.

How could I have got it so wrong? Were my words so harsh and ungracious?

What had I said that would cause this mother to think that she should stop loving her son?

The Air We Breathe

This happened almost 20 years ago. It wasn't the first time that I had spoken with concerned parents about this subject. However, it was an issue that didn't come up very often.

Today we live in a different world. Issues of same-sex attraction and gender identity are inescapable. Same-sex marriage is legal and celebrated in almost all Western countries. These days it is not uncommon to be asked what one's preferred pronouns are. Social media presents young people with a confusing range of possibilities when it comes to issues of sexual attraction and gender. A study by the Office for National Statistics found that in the UK, 10% of young people aged 16-24 identify as gay, lesbian or bisexual.

This means that more and more Christian parents find themselves in a similar position to that woman. If that includes you, I want to offer some specific help and encouragement.

This is a difficult chapter to write because parents will be coming to it with a series of specific questions stemming from a range of different situations. Is your child 14 or 44? Have they never talked to you about this, or are they in a settled same-sex relationship? Are they professing to follow Jesus, or do they make no claims to do so? Each situation will demand a different response.

In another sense, though, each situation requires the same response: the gospel of grace. A prodigal child who identifies as LGBT is not in a different category before the Lord than a prodigal child who identifies as straight. They're both lost souls in need of God's mercy—the same as you or I were before God intervened. What your child needs is not a change in their attractions or a reformation of their morals; they need to be brought to new life by God's Spirit.

All the same, parents in this situation tend to have lots of questions about how their Christian convictions intersect with their love for their children. While it is beyond the scope of this chapter to cover every possible scenario, we'll try to draw out some basic principles from Scripture and then seek to apply them in a few specific situations and conclude with some general directions.

Basic Assumptions

Before we go any further, I'll briefly lay out my basic assumptions about what the Bible teaches about gender and sexuality.

Sex is a wonderful gift from God to be enjoyed within the bounds of a marriage between one man and one woman. "God is for sex. Sex is for marriage. Marriage is for life."[5]

This foundational teaching comes from Jesus himself:

> *"Haven't you read," he replied, "that at the beginning the Creator 'made them male and female,' and said, 'For this reason a man will leave his father and mother and be united to his wife, and the two will become one flesh'?"*
>
> *(Matthew 19:4-5)*

Notice that Jesus first quotes from Genesis 1, which speaks about the fact that God created two genders, which correspond to our physical bodies (1:27). He then quotes from Genesis 2, which affirms that marriage is between a man and a woman (2:24). This is the only God-ordained context for the one-flesh sexual union.

Of course, not everyone would agree with this view. Most non-Christians would write off the Bible as archaic and irrelevant—that much is to be expected. But there is a growing number of people who would claim to be Christians but who insist that the church has misunderstood the Bible's teaching on this for most of the last 2,000 years. They argue that while the Bible condemns homosexual promiscuity, it has nothing to say about long-term loving sexual relationships between people of the same sex. Gay marriage is therefore to be celebrated. Only a capricious God would have created people who were same-sex attracted and then condemn them for seeking fulfilment in a loving relationship. How can a God of love be against love?

There are good resources available which go into these questions in more detail.[6] In this chapter, however, I want to focus on how parents might respond to an unsaved child who may be same-sex attracted or confused about their gender. But I write from the conviction that God has determined that sexual intimacy is only to be celebrated within heterosexual marriage, and that a person's birth sex and gender are the same.

I am conscious that, even among Christians who do share those convictions, not everyone will agree with the specific conclusions I come to. Many of the issues raised here are matters of wisdom and conscience. There is even debate about vocabulary. Is my son homosexual, gay or same-sex attracted? Does my daughter suffer with gender dysphoria or gender confusion, or is she transgender? I have chosen to use the phrases "same-sex attraction" and "gender confusion". There is room for a range of opinions, and we need to be charitable in the way in which we address this issue.

So let's begin with basic principles.

Five Basic Principles

1. LISTEN WELL

In our pain we may want to avoid the issue entirely. *Don't ask, don't tell.* I have met parents who have told me that they were terrified of knowing the truth. I can understand this, but I cannot see how it is beneficial in the long term. At the very least, we need to know how to pray intelligently for our children.

James puts it like this:

> *My dear brothers and sisters, take note of this: everyone should be quick to listen, slow to speak and slow to become angry, because human anger does not produce the righteousness that God desires. (James 1:19-20)*

If your child wants to talk—for the first time or for the umpteenth time—then you need to be ready to listen carefully and respond compassionately (without affirming an unbiblical lifestyle). Thank them for their honesty and the fact that they trust you enough to open up to you.

Ask questions before making pronouncements. Be curious about what's going on inside. Don't jump to conclusions about what they mean; listen to what they say. Treat them with the respect with which you would want to be treated (Matthew 7:12) and don't trivialise what they say.

2. REASSURE THEM OF YOUR LOVE

In the previous chapter, we thought about the call to love our children in Christ-like ways. This is just as true for children who experience same-sex attraction or gender confusion. In fact, they probably need even more reassurance of our love. So remind them often that you love them, that nothing they do can change that, and that you are determined that their choices will not destroy your relationship.

As in every situation, we are called to be honest, firm, kind and compassionate. Christ is our model here:

> *After this, Jesus went out and saw a tax collector by the name of Levi sitting at his tax booth. "Follow me," Jesus said to him, and Levi got up, left everything and followed him.*
>
> *Then Levi held a great banquet for Jesus at his house, and a large crowd of tax collectors and others were eating with them. But the Pharisees and the teachers of the law who belonged to their sect complained to his disciples, "Why do you eat and drink with tax collectors and sinners?"*

Jesus answered them, "It is not the healthy who need a doctor, but those who are ill. I have not come to call the righteous, but sinners to repentance." (Luke 5:27-32)

Jesus is often found in the presence of those who are considered to be "sinners". His rationale is that the whole purpose of his mission is to seek and save the lost. The irony is that his critics are blind to their own sin. They are just as much in need of a spiritual doctor as those they are criticising.

Don't put yourself in the position of Jesus' critics! You are also a sinner who depends on the grace of God. If we extend a welcome in love to our children, then they will glimpse something of the love of Christ.

3. BE COMMITTED TO THE TRUTH

In the last chapter we thought about the danger of compromising the truth in order to win our child's heart. For some, the temptation is to avoid conflict and keep the peace at all costs. Plus, I want my child to be happy—what parent doesn't? So, when they tell me that the only way they can be happy is by adopting a lifestyle which I believe to be sinful, I feel a tug in my heart. And all this is coming from the child we have loved from before they were born!

In the last chapter we also considered 1 Corinthians 13: love "does not rejoice at wrongdoing, but rejoices with the truth" (1 Corinthians 13:6, ESV). Loving someone does not mean that we should encourage them when their life choices are sinful—whether or not they are a Christians. God has expressed his will and purpose in the Scriptures. He has shown human beings how to flourish—

as individuals and as a society—and he knows and wants what is best for us. Although the Bible is clothed in a particular culture, its truths transcend all cultures, and it speaks with such a clarity as to leave us in no doubt about God's view of gender and marriage. Therefore, I cannot celebrate as "good" what God has called "bad". To do so would be dishonest; it would not be loving.

What exactly this looks like in the flow of everyday conversations and relationships is not always straightforward. But it is the line we are seeking God's help to wisely walk.

4. BE POSITIVE ABOUT GOD'S GOODNESS

The Bible celebrates God's good gift of sex. But it also makes it clear that we can live a full, rich and flourishing lives without sex. Jesus was single, as was the apostle Paul. We are human beings because we are created in the image and likeness of God. Friendship is vital to our wellbeing; but this is not true of marriage. Our world has made "sexual fulfilment" into an idol. But the Bible says that we will only find true fulfilment in relationship with God.

If your child is not a Christian, this may seem somewhat irrelevant. However, I mention it because we need our children to understand that the God we love is not mean and harsh. He is rich in grace and generous in the gifts that he gives to us. James tells us:

> *Don't be deceived, my dear brothers and sisters. Every good and perfect gift is from above, coming down from the Father of the heavenly lights, who does not change like shifting shadows. (James 1:16-17)*

Do I really believe that God is good all the way through? Our children are unlikely to believe that God is good if we are not persuaded ourselves.

So take every opportunity you can to talk about the goodness God—in all areas of your life. He is abundantly generous! Make this the dominant tone of your conversations. Our children should hear more from us about what God is for—beauty, goodness, justice, kindness—than what he is against. And create opportunities to enjoy God's good world together with your children: food, music, art, the outdoors. We are not called to be killjoys!

5. BE HUMBLE ABOUT THE CAUSES

There is a contentious debate about why some people experience same-sex attraction. Is it "nature" or "nurture"? Is it the result of living in a broken world where we are all damaged because of the curse of sin? Is there such a thing as a gay gene?

Similar questions surround the causes of gender confusion. Is it a form of illness or an act of rebellion? Is it an expression of same-sex attraction or an autistic-spectrum disorder, or is it primarily the result of adolescent confusion or peer pressure?

Christians do not agree, and we would be unwise to be dogmatic. But however we understand the cause, we cannot attribute any blame to God. James writes:

> *When tempted, no one should say, "God is tempting me." For God cannot be tempted by evil, nor does he tempt anyone; but each person is tempted when they are dragged away by their own evil desire and enticed.*
>
> *(James 1:13-14)*

God cannot be responsible for sin. We are responsible for our own actions. We cannot use genetics or circumstances or anything else as an excuse for behaviour that contradicts God's revealed will in Scripture.

We have already explored the fact that if our children are not saved, it's quite easy to blame ourselves and to be tortured with a sense of guilt. This may be particularly all-consuming if we believe that our child's sexuality is the result of our failure as parents. There are plenty of theories out there along these lines: perhaps the father was too distant, or the mother was too domineering.

However, all of this is purely speculative, and it is certainly not helpful to go hunting in the past for causes. As we have said repeatedly, none of us are perfect parents, and we have to look to God's grace to cover our failures—and trust that he is powerful enough to save our prodigal children.

Three Different Scenarios

Let's try to apply these principles to three different scenarios.

SCENARIO ONE

You are the parent of a teenager who is same-sex attracted or questioning their gender identity. They are confused and anxious, but they want to talk with you about it.

You may have had suspicions already, or you may have been completely in the dark. Both you and they will probably find the situation very embarrassing, but it is important that you make it as easy as possible for them to approach you. As difficult as it is, you need to know the truth.

They may come to you in fear and trembling—they love you, and they know that what they say will hurt you. Or they may approach you with bravado or even an arrogant defiance.

Whatever their attitude, first, listen well. Ask open questions: "How long have you felt this way?" or "How can I help you?" Listen carefully to the words that they're using. Are they struggling with the temptation of same-sex attraction, or have they decided that being gay or transgender is their identity? Are they making a declaration, or are they asking for assistance? And where does God figure in their thinking? For many young people, the real issue is one of confusion and fear. They have experienced feelings which they cannot really understand, and they are struggling with adolescent angst. For some children, this is simply a phase which may quickly pass. For others, it isn't. At this point, you can't tell for sure. So, however you read the situation, treat them with respect and don't trivialise what they say.

Second, reassure them of your love. It would be difficult to labour this point too much!

Third, speak God's truth and goodness. Resist the temptation to launch into lecture mode. Ask them what they think God thinks about this. They may know the right answers already; or you may be surprised by what they've misunderstood. But be clear. You cannot make it easy for them by pretending that it doesn't matter; it does matter. Pretending otherwise would be dishonest and detrimental to them. But be clear about God's grace too; they are not too far gone from him. Tell them the gospel. It is when we feel at our most messed-up that these truths shine most brightly.

This is not a one-time conversation (but nor is it something you need to bring up at every dinner). So keep the channels of communication open. While it is important that your child feels that they can talk with you, it is also true that you are so close to them that it may be quite difficult to be objective in what you say. They may benefit from talking with someone else outside the situation. If you suggest this, make sure that they don't think that you are rejecting them.

SCENARIO TWO

You are the parent of a young adult who is "out", who professes to follow Jesus and says that the Bible affirms their right to a same-sex sexual relationship.

Again, ask plenty of questions and listen carefully to what they say. Are they really convinced of their position, or are they confused? Who is influencing them? How did they come to this position?

Their arguments may seem to be powerful and persuasive:

> *How can you be so mean and so unkind? I only want to be happy! I thought you loved me!*
>
> *I thought you said that Jesus wants us to love each other. You are behaving like one of those Pharisees!*
>
> *You've got it wrong. There's a church near my university where they welcome gay people and do gay weddings. They love Jesus, and they don't reject me like you do.*
>
> *Since I came out, I've joined a group on campus who accept me as I really am. I don't have to pretend anymore.*

Don't try and duck the arguments. Take them back to some of the biblical truths outlined above. You may point them to books on the subject which are both biblically faithful and accessible. You may seek help from someone who has more experience. Don't be afraid to ask for help from Christian groups which minister into this area.[7]

Once again, do everything in love. Be careful not to become aggressive in the way in which you respond to their arguments. The pain we feel may cause us to lash out. This will be detrimental. Remember that however confident your child sounds, there may be great fear and insecurity lying beneath the surface. Reiterate that everything you say is coming from a place of deep love for them.

At the same time, they need to understand the danger that they are in. Groups who teach that the Bible is comfortable with a same-sex relationship will probably also downplay the reality of judgment and hell. The Bible teaches that unrepentant sexual sinners will not inherit the kingdom of God (1 Corinthians 6:9-10). Nothing is beyond forgiveness—but you cannot repent of something that you do not consider to be sin.

SCENARIO THREE

You are the parent of an adult who makes no claims to follow Jesus, has been living an openly LGBT lifestyle for several years, and is in a serious same-sex relationship.

If this is a situation your family has been living with for a while, it's easy to lose hope. But with God there is always hope. So keep praying; keep loving your child with your words and actions; keep seeking opportunities to share something of the gospel with them. As in the previous scenario, it would be right to remind them from time to time of the seriousness of their spiritual situation.

Another real danger is that as time goes by, we accept a "new normal". The same-sex relationship has lasted for a long time, and both partners seem to be happy and faithful. We just want to keep the peace. I have met parents who have told me that they have been tempted to change their view of what the Bible teaches because of this scenario.

It is important that this does not compromise our faith in any way. Our children should know what we think—even if what we think of their lifestyle doesn't need to come up in every conversation.

This situation will throw up a host of more specific questions. How do you respond when they want to introduce you to their partner? Should you be willing to meet them, or do you refuse to have any contact? If you agree to meet, do you meet on neutral ground or do you invite them into your home? What happens if they want to take part in a family celebration or to join a family holiday? Should you go to a child's same-sex wedding?

I don't have a definitive answer to any of these questions. The truth is that Christians come to different conclusions and respond in different ways. In each case we have to exercise biblical wisdom and avoid judging each other on the choices we make. Pray earnestly, and seek the counsel of your pastor or a wise Christian friend.

Do your best to present a united front with your spouse. I remember one couple I spoke to who struggled over attending the celebration of their son's wedding to his gay partner. One of them was adamant that this was a step too far and that they could not celebrate something which God did not approve of. The other one was terrified that not attending gave the impression that they wanted nothing more to do with their son. Don't allow anything to drive a wedge between you.

Three Final Thoughts

1. REACH OUT FOR HELP

> *What on earth would they think of me at church if they knew how my daughter was living? When I see all the happy families around me, I feel like a freak and a failure and a phony. Isn't it better to suffer in silence and pretend that things are fine?*

Not everyone needs to know about your situation, but you should not be afraid to ask for help. Depending on the specifics, you may decide to share your burden with a small group of close and trusted friends while keeping the circle of knowledge tight, both for your own sake and for the sake of your child.

Churches need to work hard at being the kinds of communities that God wants them to be. We are all sinners saved by grace, and yet we find it easy to look down on certain expressions of sin as "worse" than others. When we do that, we begin to think like the Pharisee in Jesus' parable:

> *The Pharisee stood by himself and prayed: "God, I thank you that I am not like other people—robbers, evildoers, adulterers—or even like this tax collector." (Luke 18:11)*

This should not be so. Almost every Christian battles with sexual temptation. If we remember that, parents in pain can benefit from the essential encouragement and support that only a compassionate church family can bring.

2. LEARN TO MOURN

The Bible celebrates both marriage and singleness. Next to their child's conversion, many parents' biggest hope is that they will find a loving partner and be able to raise a family. I want to be a grandparent! But, if they remain single, I want them to enjoy all the blessings of singleness. However, if our children try to live outside God's boundaries, they can never experience the fulfilment which he offers. This should cause us to grieve.

But for some parents it is even worse.

I have counselled parents who now have no contact at all with their adult children. There is an empty place at the table on Christmas Day. Texts and phone calls are ignored. Someone once said to me…

It feels as if my daughter is dead.

Perhaps that's you. In this situation it is important to be honest with God and to pour out our hearts in grief before him. Remember that he is the God who comforts those who grieve and who "heals the broken-hearted and binds up their wounds" (Psalm 147:3).

3. BE HOPEFUL ABOUT GRACE

It bears repeating that the fact that your child identifies as LGBT is only the presenting problem. The greater problem is that they don't know Jesus. That means that the real solution is not first that they abandon a sinful lifestyle but that they turn to Christ. The answer is always the gospel.

Homosexual sin is not the unforgivable sin. In one of most often quoted passages on this subject, the apostle Paul writes:

> *Or do you not know that wrongdoers will not inherit the kingdom of God? Do not be deceived: neither the sexually immoral nor idolaters nor adulterers nor men who have sex with men nor thieves nor the greedy nor drunkards nor slanderers nor swindlers will inherit the kingdom of God. (1 Corinthians 6:9-10)*

Notice how same-sex sex is not singled out for special treatment but is placed alongside "respectable sins" like greed or slander. All of them place us outside of the kingdom of God if we persist in them without repentance. Yet the answer to all of these sins is the glorious grace of God, which comes to us in the gospel. Paul goes on:

> *And that is what some of you were. But you were washed, you were sanctified, you were justified in the name of the Lord Jesus Christ and by the Spirit of our God. (v 11)*

We sometimes imagine that some people, because of their temperament or life circumstances, are naturally closer to accepting the gospel than others. We think that it will be harder, if not impossible, for God to save my same-sex attracted son or my gender-confused daughter. This is not true. Every conversion is a miracle. God can overcome any barrier. He did it in Corinth. He can do it in your family.

In the gospel God not only offers us forgiveness and grace, but he also offers us the power to change. Christians have different experiences of freedom from the power of sin. For many people who experience same-sex attraction, Christian faithfulness will mean a life of sexual abstinence. God gives grace to enable faithfulness in this situation. Others enter into a heterosexual marriage which, again by God's grace, becomes a place of flourishing.[8] We cannot predict how God will work in any particular situation—but we can have confidence in the power of the gospel to transform any heart.

No one is too difficult for God.

But while I wait, it still hurts. What am I to do with my pain? We will try to answer this question in the next chapter.

QUESTIONS

1. This chapter talked about listening, loving, and speaking truth. How do we get the balance right? What happens if we don't?
2. What do we mean when we talk about the goodness of God? Why is it important that we impress this truth upon our children?
3. It is very important how we communicate with our children, particularly on these subjects. Read Ephesians 4:25-32. What does Paul tell us here about the art of good communication?
4. How can we help parents deal with the sense of guilt which is associated with the subject of this chapter?

CHAPTER 8

CAN I GROW THROUGH THE PAIN?

What Are You Praying For?

I once heard a speaker at a conference share how, when he had been a young pastor of a small church, there had been a lady in his congregation who was passing through a time of intense trial. She suffered from a whole raft of serious ailments. At the same time, she was nursing a house-bound, terminally ill husband. It was nearly impossible for her to get to church, but one Sunday evening, thanks to the kindness of Christian friends, she made it. When the pastor stood to preach, his heart was warmed to see her sitting on the back row. At the close of the service, it was obvious that she was anxious to get home quickly. He rushed to the back and caught her just as she was leaving the building. He grasped her hand and thanked her for her attendance and assured her that he was praying for her and her husband.

She stopped and looked quizzically into his eyes:

Well, thank you, pastor. Do you mind if I ask you a question? What are you praying for?

The pastor's mind went blank. He mouthed a few banalities and felt very embarrassed. Still holding his hand, the lady smiled and spoke again:

If you don't mind, can I tell you what to pray? Please pray that my husband and I don't waste this trial. Ask for help to discern God's purpose and be faithful to it.[9]

Having unsaved children is its own sort of trial. Do we, like that woman, believe that God has purposes for the pain? Can we pray for ourselves that the Lord might use our pain for his work in our lives and also in the lives of others?

That might sound almost impossible; can fruit really flourish in the soil of a broken heart?

How can we avoid wasting our suffering and our disappointments?

We will explore the answer to these questions in the course of this chapter.

Learn to Lament

The place to begin is by acknowledging that something is profoundly wrong when our kids reject Christ.

At first the temptation is to ignore it. "Of course my children are saved," we tell ourselves. "This is just a blip." And that may be the case. But after a time, we eventually come to the conclusion that our children are no longer disciples of Jesus. If we take that fact seriously, we need to lament. Grief is the unavoidable reaction to loss or significant change, and there are few experiences of loss greater than this. It feels like a bereavement—and the biblical response to bereavement is to lament.

There are 150 psalms in the Bible, and at least 50 may be described as laments.[10] In these psalms, the author pours out his heart before God. They begin in the darkness but usually end in the light. They move from fear and perplexity and pain to faith and hope and confidence.

Take Psalm 13 as an example. David begins by deliberately turning to the Lord and pouring out his heart to him in desperate urgency—struggling with both God's apparent inactivity and his own pain.

> *How long, Lord? Will you forget me for ever?*
> *How long will you hide your face from me?*
> *How long must I wrestle with my thoughts*
> *and day after day have sorrow in my heart?*
> *How long will my enemy triumph over me?*
> *(Psalm 13:1-2)*

We do not know when David wrote this psalm, but it was clearly at a time when he was under pressure from his enemies. The anguish described here finds its fullest fulfilment in the experience of Jesus, the Man of Sorrows. However, David's cries also resonate with parents in pain.

Why did God give you the blessing of children and then break your heart when those children turned their back on him? Why is he so slow to answer your prayers? You have asked for your children to be brought back to Christ, but instead they seem to be moving further from him. Does God really hear your prayers? Suffering is so lonely!

But David does not despair. His desperate cry becomes a passionate prayer:

Look on me and answer, LORD my God.
Give light to my eyes, or I will sleep in death,
and my enemy will say, "I have overcome him,"
and my foes will rejoice when I fall. (Psalm 13:3-4)

Notice again that although David's circumstances are very different from your own, David's example is one that you can follow. You may not fear that your enemies will triumph or that they will rob you of your life. But you are filled with anxious fears about your children and their eternal destiny. And so, like David, you can deliberately cast yourself on God and pray that he might look upon you and answer your cries.

Notice how there is a change in David's heart as he reaches out to God in humility. This is why laments do not lead to despair:

Despair lives under the hopeless resignation that God doesn't care, he doesn't hear, and nothing is ever going to change.[11]

Lament, on the other hand, moves from despair to hope. We have a faithful Father, and we can approach his throne "in our time of need" (Hebrew 4:16).

And so the psalm ends with a confession of trust:

But I trust in your unfailing love;
my heart rejoices in your salvation.
I will sing the LORD's praise,
for he has been good to me. (v 5-6)

Faith grows and hope is reborn as you honestly confess your needs to God. And this faith is more than intellectual assent. It involves trust:

> *Trust is not a passive state of mind. It is a vigorous act of the soul by which we choose to lay hold on the promises of God and cling to them despite the adversity that at times seeks to overwhelm us.*[12]

In this sense, lamenting involves a journey—a journey from desolation to delight. Often the circumstances which provoked the lament have not changed, but the heart of the one lamenting has been renewed. As you lament, you begin to see things differently. Your children may still be a long way from God, but your perspective has changed.

Lamentation is not the same as unbelief or grumbling. When you lament, you are bringing your grief to God and expressing your emotions in a healthy way. And when you do this, you discover God's steadfast love and fatherly compassion. You do not need to pretend to be strong. God delights to bless us in our weakness because it is here that his strength is made known.

So follow David's pattern. Cry out to God with your grief. Be honest with him about how you really feel. Plead with him to act on your behalf. Then declare your trust in his love and goodness.

And remember that lament is not a one-and-done thing. Your child may have been wandering from the Lord for 20 years. It is still a good thing to bring your pain to the Lord in lament from time to time. You may grow weary of praying. He never grows weary of listening!

The Purpose of Pain

Every day we are surrounded by voices which may promise to bring some immediate relief to our pain but in the end only offer powerless placebos. It's easy to be led by our chaotic emotions or the soothing suggestions of false friends. However, if your children are not Christians, they are lost—and the hurt you feel is not a phantom pain but real and genuine.

This is the truth. But it is also true that God has a purpose in the pain. God rules over all things and works all things for the good of those who love him (Romans 8:28). God's actions are determined by his character, which means that what he does is always good:

He is the Rock, his works are perfect,
and all his ways are just.
A faithful God who does no wrong,
upright and just is he. (Deuteronomy 32:4)

Our problem is that we just can't figure it out. We are limited in our understanding, and we cannot see how what God is doing in our lives can be described as good. So, to help focus your eyes of faith, here are three ways in which the grief we feel for our prodigal children can lead to blessing.

1. IT DRIVES US INTO THE ARMS OF GOD

The supreme purpose of our lives is to know God. We have been created to glorify him and to enjoy him for ever. This is both our intended purpose and our ultimate destiny (Genesis 3:8; Revelation 22:4). When things are going well, we often lose sight of this. But when we struggle with a situation we can't change, we are driven into the arms of God.

Self-reliance is the enemy of faith. Suffering forces us to rely on God, not ourselves. Trials magnify God's grace in our lives and help us to recognise our dependence on him. Paul had come to realise this, and so he writes to the Christians at Corinth:

> *We do not want you to be uninformed, brothers and sisters, about the troubles we experienced in the province of Asia. We were under great pressure, far beyond our ability to endure, so that we despaired of life itself. Indeed, we felt we had received the sentence of death. But this happened that we might not rely on ourselves but on God, who raises the dead. (2 Corinthians 1:8-9)*

Paul's pain was pushing him beyond himself and into a deeper fellowship with God. My friends Jake and Amanda had a similar experience. This lovely couple had two delightful daughters and a son who broke their heart. One day, when, once again, his drug habit had resulted in a visit from the police, they asked to see me. We talked and prayed and wept together. Then, quoting something that he had heard in a sermon, Jake told me:

> *I don't know what we would do if we didn't have the Lord. You only come to know that God is all you need when God is all you've got.*

Jake and Amanda's dependence upon God was palpable.

Paul returns to this subject later in his letter when he describes his "thorn in [the] flesh" (2 Corinthians 12:7). The thorn was a painful, chronic, limiting and humiliating problem (although we're not told exactly what). Paul prayed earnestly for its removal, not only because of the agony he felt but also because it seemed to him that it was limiting the effectiveness of his ministry.

I have talked to pastors and church leaders who have described their prodigal children in these terms. Some have even considered abandoning ministry because of the guilt that they feel. If only their thorn was removed—if only their child was converted—they might be able to preach more effectively and lead God's flock more effectively.

But for Paul this was not God's plan. In response to his pleas, the Lord told him:

> *My grace is sufficient for you, for my power is made perfect in weakness. (v 9)*

Paul responds:

> *Therefore I will boast all the more gladly about my weaknesses, so that Christ's power may rest on me. That is why, for Christ's sake, I delight in weaknesses, in insults, in hardships, in persecutions, in difficulties. For when I am weak, then I am strong. (v 9-10)*

It is easy to drift from God. We can be diligent in our religion and distant in our relationship. Yet the pain caused by a prodigal child creates within our heart a longing for the parental love which only God can give. Let your pain drive you into his arms.

2. IT STRIPS AWAY THE IDOLS OF OUR HEARTS

In the Bible, the heart is the driving force behind our thoughts and deeds, our desires and decisions, our affections and actions. It represents the whole of us, and we are commanded to guard it:

> *Above all else, guard your heart,*
> *for everything you do flows from it. (Proverbs 4:23)*

The problem is that our hearts are often under siege. Instead of loving God with all our heart, we find ourselves enamoured with and captivated by other things. The Bible refers to these "other things" as idols. God informed his servant Ezekiel that this was the basic problem among the people of Israel:

> *Son of man, these men have set up idols in their hearts and put wicked stumbling-blocks before their faces.*
>
> *(Ezekiel 14:3)*

Sin is not only doing bad things; it is also making good things into ultimate things. We prize good things more than we prize God. Idols are stunningly diverse and include such things as money, power, education, work, appearance, a spouse—anything besides God that we crave and think we cannot live without.

And among these idols is, of course, our children. Children are a blessing from God, but we can come to delight more in the gift than in the Giver. In a subtle way, we begin to build our lives around them before God. We listen to their voices and are afraid of offending them. If they're not happy in the youth group, we consider trying another church. When they want to play football on a Sunday morning, we prioritise that over meeting with God's people in worship. We imagine that our sacrifices will ensure their salvation, but when they reject the faith, we are devastated. This is clearly a caricature, but it should raise important questions. In a clear choice between pleasing God and pleasing my children, what will determine my decisions?

Or perhaps, if you're honest, it's less about your children and more about you. It's being seen as "a good parent" that matters to you most. You were the family that always did the right things. When your kids were younger, your parenting was admired by peers at church. Other people came to you for advice on handling difficult teenagers or doing family Bible times. But now one of your own children has walked away, and in your wounded pride, you realise how much "being a good parent" meant to you all along.

Loss is designed to reveal the problems of our heart. Am I willing to love Jesus more than I love my idols? Can I surrender them to him? Do I see my children as on loan? If they are never saved in my lifetime, will this destroy my trust in and my love for God?

Will we be like Job? After a day of disasters, there is one last piece of bad news:

> *Yet another messenger came and said, "Your sons and daughters were feasting and drinking wine at the eldest brother's house, when suddenly a mighty wind swept in from the desert and struck the four corners of the house. It collapsed on them and they are dead, and I am the only one who has escaped to tell you!" (Job 1:18-19)*

How does Job respond?

> *At this, Job got up and tore his robe and shaved his head. Then he fell to the ground in worship and said:*
>
> *"Naked I came from my mother's womb,*
> *and naked I shall depart.*
> *The LORD gave and the LORD has taken away;*
> *may the name of the LORD be praised."*
>
> *In all this, Job did not sin by charging God with wrongdoing. (v 20-22)*

I'm sure that Job loved his children, but he knew that they were a gift from God, and he was willing to surrender them to God. Are we willing to do the same with our children?

3. IT TRANSFORMS US INTO THE LIKENESS OF CHRIST

God is committed to making us holy:

> *But just as he who called you is holy, so be holy in all you do; for it is written: "Be holy, because I am holy."*
>
> *(1 Peter 1:15-16)*

The greatest thing God does today is to take a sinful man or woman out of a sinful world, make them holy, put them back in a sinful world and keep them holy. But holiness is not some weird kind of pietism that strips us of our humanity. The model for holiness is the character of Jesus, the most perfectly balanced and wonderfully human person who has ever lived. Kevin DeYoung captures this beautifully in his book *The Hole in Our Holiness*:

> *We see all the virtues of holiness perfectly aligned in Christ.*
>
> *He was always gentle, but never soft.*
>
> *He was bold but never brash.*
>
> *He was pure but never prudish.*
>
> *He was full of mercy but never at the expense of justice.*
>
> *He was full of truth but not at the expense of grace.*
>
> *In everything he was submissive to his Father, and he gave everything for his sheep.*
>
> *He obeyed his parents, kept the law of God, and forgave his enemies.*

> *He never lusted, never coveted and never lied.*
>
> *In all that Jesus Christ did, during his whole life and especially as his life came to an end, he loved God with his whole being and loved his neighbour as himself.*
>
> *If somewhere down the road you forget the Ten Commandments or can't recall the fruit of the Spirit or don't remember any particular attribute of God, you can still remember what holiness is by simply remembering his name.*[13]

This is who God is making us like. He uses the Bible, people and circumstances to do it. But he also uses suffering. Jesus learned obedience through what he suffered (Hebrews 5:8), and so do we. God is building character—and character usually develops in times of adversity. And watching our children turn their back on God is a profound adversity. Seeking to love children who do not love Jesus shapes our character and deepens our likeness to Christ.

But we need a word of caution here. Suffering can make us better, or it can also make us bitter. We can descend into a whirlpool of self-pity, grief, guilt, fear and blame. Or we can look beyond the pain, remember God's grace, see the purpose and count it all joy (James 1:2-4). How we respond to suffering makes all the difference—and how we respond depends on us.

Are you wasting your suffering?

QUESTIONS

1. Read 2 Corinthians 1:3-7. One way of making sure that we do not waste our suffering is to be available to help others in theirs. How might you comfort other parents in pain with the comfort you have received?
2. What was new to you in the section on lament? What might be some of the dangers if we don't turn our pain into lament?
3. Are there ways in which your experience of loving a prodigal child has deepened your reliance on God or revealed idols in your heart?
4. "Suffering can make us better, or it can also make us ... How we respond to suffering makes all the difference—and how we respond depends on us." How can we make sure that we respond in the right way to the heartbreak caused by prodigal children?

CHAPTER 9

WHAT ABOUT...?

Perplexing Questions

During most of my ministry, I regularly held what I grandly called a "weekly surgery". It was an opportunity for people to come and talk with me without a prearranged appointment. Sometimes they were seeking advice or wanting prayer. Very often, they came with questions that were perplexing them. Increasingly over the years, these questions centred on the heartache caused by prodigal children.

I hope that I have dealt with most of these in the course of this book. However, there are three issues that we have not yet touched on. It may be that the questions raised here have never occurred, but in my experience, they are more common than you might imagine. So do read on—in the future, you may find yourself trying to help a parent with one of these concerns.

1. What If My Child Has Committed the Unforgivable Sin?

I will call him Peter, although that was not his name. For several months, we met together irregularly to pray for his son's conversion. Steve had professed faith and had been baptised, and was fully engaged in the university student group. He was a bright lad who knew the Bible well and was theologically informed. But after graduation, he seemed to drift away from church and eventually told his dad that he was no longer interested in following Jesus.

Peter and I had been praying together for Steve for several weeks when one day he came into my study looking deeply troubled:

> *I have just been reading about the unforgivable sin. What if Steve has committed that sin? What's the point of praying for him when Jesus says there's no hope for forgiveness? What do you think?*

The passage to which he referred was the words of Jesus when he was responding to accusations that his power to cast out evil spirits had been derived from the devil. Here, Jesus offers forgiveness, but he warns that those who deliberately misrepresent the work of the Holy Spirit are in danger of committing a sin which cannot be forgiven:

> *And so I tell you, every kind of sin and slander can be forgiven, but blasphemy against the Spirit will not be forgiven. Anyone who speaks a word against the Son of Man will be forgiven, but anyone who speaks against the Holy Spirit will not be forgiven, either in this age or in the age to come. (Matthew 12:31-32)*

Although Jesus does not give a specific definition of "blasphemy against the Spirit", it appears to be more than just unbelief. It is a determined and stubborn refusal to believe despite the overwhelming evidence. These men had seen the clear evidence of Jesus' identity in the way in which he had defeated the powers of the devil and set men free from evil spirits, but they were resolute in their refusal to believe that Jesus is God. Instead, they attributed the work of God to Satan.

The Holy Spirit continues to bear witness to Jesus today. Those who wilfully and slanderously reject his testimony are in danger of committing this sin.

Later in the New Testament, we find references to other sins which seem to fall into the same category. The book of Hebrews says:

> *It is impossible for those who have once been enlightened, who have tasted the heavenly gift, who have shared in the Holy Spirit, who have tasted the goodness of the word of God and the powers of the coming age and who have fallen away, to be brought back to repentance. To their loss they are crucifying the Son of God all over again and subjecting him to public disgrace. (Hebrews 6:4-6)*

And again:

> *If we deliberately keep on sinning after we have received the knowledge of the truth, no sacrifice for sins is left, but only a fearful expectation of judgment and of raging fire that will consume the enemies of God. (10:26-27)*

These words trouble Christian parents because they describe the sin of those who have been on the inside of the Christian faith. Children brought up in a Christian home know the truth. In some ways, they have "been enlightened" and "have tasted the heavenly gift". They may well have made a profession of faith, but now they are denying it.

Putting the passages together, it seems that the "unforgivable sin" involves the conscious, malicious and wilful rejection of Christ, coupled with the deliberate slandering of the truth of the gospel and attributing the work of God to Satan. It involves both illumination and malice, and it leads to a conscious and consistently proclaimed hatred of God. The reason that it cannot be forgiven is that it deadens the conscience and hardens the sinner. The person loses their moral compass, and rather than rejoicing in the truth, they come to hate it.

Can you understand Peter's fear? Steve had a more-than-average knowledge of the Bible, yet in his words and deeds, he had rejected the gospel.

So what can we say? Well, we have to take the warnings of these passages seriously, but it is not our place to apply them to any particular individual. We do not know a person's heart. The evidence that someone has committed this sin is that they persist aggressively in denying and denouncing the gospel. But the moment that such a person has any desire to turn from their sin, Christ is always ready and willing to forgive—their repentance would be evidence that they had not, in fact, crossed into the unforgivable sin. So, along with hearing Scripture's warning, we should be assured that there is always a way back to God should our children choose to use it.

My advice to Peter was that we should not speculate but rather continue to pray, recognising that no one is too difficult for God. It might be appropriate for Peter to warn his son about the danger of a hardened conscience, but in the end, we have to give our children to God and to leave the matter with him.

Let me add just one afterthought. When I was at school, one of my Christian friends became very angry with God when his dad died suddenly and unexpectedly. In his bitterness, he denounced his faith and, quoting the passages from Hebrews, told me that he had committed the unforgivable sin and that there was no point in my praying for him to return to God. It was too late. He was lost for ever.

I have to confess that I was shocked and confused. But I didn't stop praying. After we both left school, I lost contact with this friend for over 20 years. But one day, speaking as the visiting preacher at the morning service of a little baptist church, I noticed a familiar face a few rows back. It was my friend from school. He was a little embarrassed when we talked together after the service but confessed that after several years in a spiritual wilderness, he had returned home to his Father's house and found that his Father joyfully received him. There is hope for your child yet.

2. Should I Be a Church Leader Or an Elder If My Children Are Unsaved?

Healthy churches are led by healthy Christian leaders. In his letter to Timothy, the apostle Paul gives a list of qualifications to look for in potential elders. This includes the following:

> *He must manage his own family well and see that his children obey him, and he must do so in a manner worthy of full respect. (If anyone does not know how to manage his own family, how can he take care of God's church?) (1 Timothy 3:4-5)*

However, this does not suggest that an elder's children must be Christians, but that while they're at home, they should be obedient and treat their parents with respect.

Fathers had absolute authority over their children in the 1st century, when Paul was writing. We live in a different culture, where young adults enjoy greater freedom from their parents. So, a faithful application of these verses today would apply them to the period when the child is still at home and under parental care. Things may be complicated because of conditions such as autism. However, church leaders should manage their families wisely, even when there are complications. If the home is marked by a chaotic lack of discipline and the children are behaving in a wild and disrespectful way, this would disqualify their parent from leadership within the church. This seems to make sense. The former minister John Stott put it like this:

> *The married pastor is called to leadership in two families, his and God's, and the former is to be the training ground of the latter.*[14]

Again, Paul says nothing here about the child becoming a Christian, which of course is not in the gift of their parents anyway! So, from these verses, it seems clear that having unconverted children does not disqualify someone from church leadership.

However, the situation seems more complicated when we look at what Paul wrote to Titus:

> *An elder must be blameless, faithful to his wife, a man whose children believe and are not open to the charge of being wild and disobedient. (Titus 1:6)*

Some argue that this verse teaches that if an elder's child deserts the faith, either doctrinally or morally, the parent must step down from church leadership.

Is this correct? Is Paul adding an additional qualification for leadership to the list found in 1 Timothy?

I have walked through the situation with church leaders who have experienced the intense pain of a child who has turned away from the faith and made shipwreck of their lives. Does this mean they have failed in their parenting and need to step back from their ministry?

The answer to all these questions is "no".

The most natural assumption is that Paul is saying the same thing to Titus as he was saying to Timothy, but in a slightly different way. The word "believe" in Titus 1:6 could also be translated "faithful" or "trustworthy". The context must decide which translation is the best fit, and the context here defines the word in behavioural terms—"not open to the charge of being wild and disobedient". This is not a statement about salvation—just as in 1 Timothy, Paul is referring to the submission and obedience of an elder's children, not whether they have come to faith.

As we saw in an earlier chapter, if a dad sets a good example and leads his home with wise and gentle discipline, we would expect that his children will be obedient. That's because obedient behaviour does not require miraculous intervention—whereas salvation does. While a godly home is often conducive to belief, it does not produce it. If we insist that a child's salvation is fundamentally connected to the managerial skills of their parents, we have inadvertently assigned an unbiblical role to human action. We cannot convert our children, but we can and should control their behaviour when they are under our roof. If, while under our authority, our children are rebellious, then we are disqualified from ministry. Paul is not asking any more of the elder and his children than is expected of every Christian father and his children.

3. How Can I Enjoy Heaven If My Children Are Not There?

This must be the most heart-wrenching question of all.

Those who trust in Christ are rescued from future judgment and enter into the secure and certain hope of eternal bliss in God's presence.

But those who die outside of Christ are lost. Nominal faith will not suffice. Jesus says:

> *Not everyone who says to me, "Lord, Lord," will enter the kingdom of heaven, but only the one who does the will of my Father who is in heaven. Many will say to me on that day, "Lord, Lord, did we not prophesy in your name and in your name drive out demons and in your name perform many miracles?" Then I will tell them plainly, "I never knew you. Away from me, you evildoers!" (Matthew 7:21-23)*

It is impossible to deny the existence of hell and remain faithful to the teaching of Jesus. But how can I possibly enjoy heaven if the people I love most in this world are not there? More than that, how can I enjoy it when I know that those people are experiencing God's eternal judgment?

The question is often raised by new Christians who have lost a parent or a partner. I think of Pam, who came along to church after the death of her husband, Derek. One day, she asked to see me.

> *I understand what you teach. I want to trust Jesus. But one thing holds me back. I loved Derek, and I miss him every day. I want to know where I am going to go when I die—but if Derek isn't in heaven, I'm not sure I want to go there.*

This is also an intensely agonising question for those who have lost a child. What if my daughter showed no evidence of faith when she died? What if my son committed suicide?[15]

How do we respond to this?

The first thing to say is that we must not give false hope. Only those who have come to Christ in faith will be saved. When a child has made a profession of faith at an early age but no longer lives as a Christian, you sometimes hear people say that they are saved "but not walking with the Lord at the moment". This may well be the case. But true saving faith is accompanied by the evidence of persistent Christian discipleship. The apostle John gets the balance right:

> *We know that anyone born of God does not continue to sin; the One who was born of God keeps them safe, and the evil one cannot harm them. (1 John 5:18)*

A true believer is "born of God" and cannot continue sinning as if sin didn't matter. None of us will ever reach sinless perfection (1:8 – 2:1), but we can never be a "happy sinner". However, if a child has been truly saved, then Christ, the one who was born of God in a unique way, will keep them safe and protect them from the devil.

The second thing to affirm is that we do not know the state of anyone's soul, even at the end of their lives. We cannot know the ultimate destination of an individual. Only God can judge and truly know a person's heart. We can know that God is utterly just and never makes a wrong judgment. The God of the earth will do what is right (Genesis 18:25). I think that the hardest thing we ever have to do is to give our children to God and then leave them with him. Speculating where they might be is unhelpful. Surrendering them to the God who loves us and knows our broken hearts is our only alternative.

Finally, if you worry that you won't be happy in heaven if your child is not there, remember that God himself will wipe away all tears from your eyes (Revelation 21:4). If you weep now, that is only to be expected. We live in the midst of a vale of tears. In heaven, all mourning and grief will be gone for ever. You will see with a new and clearer perspective. Like the angels, you will delight in God's perfect goodness and justice. At the same time, you will be amazed at grace and astonished that God, in justice, would punish his own Son to rescue you from hell. Your salvation will be a cause of eternal gratitude.

I may not be able to give you a full and satisfying answer now, but I know that in heaven, God's presence will wash away all your pain.

But of course, many of the people we love are still alive. If they are not saved, we must do all in our power to win them for Christ. Pray and weep and speak. Point them to Christ and trust that God hears.

Don't give up!

And remember that you don't have to do this on your own. Your brothers and sisters in Christ are there to help you. How? Read on!

QUESTIONS

1. Are the questions in this chapter ones that you have wrestled with? Do you know someone else with these concerns?

2. Is it ever right to stop praying for the conversion of our children? How do these Bible verses help us to answer this question? Luke 11:5-10; 1 Thessalonians 5:17; Hebrews 4:16.

3. Someone once said, "Leaders should be model parents. Their children shouldn't necessarily be model children." Is this true? If so, how should we understand and apply it either as leaders or those who pray for their leaders?

4. When we suffer, we need compassion, truth and hope. What comfort could you offer to a friend who thinks that their child died without knowing Christ?

CHAPTER 10

HOW CAN WE HELP?

Everybody Hurts

Imagine your church on Sunday morning. Scan the room in your mind's eye. How many different griefs or trials do you see people carrying? There are likely to be dozens or even scores of them, depending on the size of your church. In this broken world, the only pre-condition for suffering is to live long enough.

This truth is found on almost every page of the Bible. If you pinch out the first two chapters of Genesis and the last two chapters of Revelation, then suffering and pain is the common theme of everything in between. The human race came from a pain-free zone where everything was "very good" (Genesis 1:31). God's people are heading for a pain-free zone when all things will be made new and the curse of sin and all its consequences will be gone for ever (Revelation 21:5). However, we are not there yet. We live in the middle of the book, and this is marked by tears and death and mourning and crying and pain (v 4).

We live in a fallen, broken and bleeding world:

We know that the whole creation has been groaning as in the pains of childbirth right up to the present time. Not only so, but we ourselves, who have the firstfruits of the Spirit, groan inwardly as we wait eagerly for our adoption to sonship, the redemption of our bodies.
(Romans 8:22-23)

We struggle because we are human, but we also struggle because we are Christians. Most of the references to suffering in the New Testament are related to the cost of discipleship. We suffer because we follow in the footsteps of our crucified Saviour. And the heartbreak of parenting unsaved children is part of the price of faithfulness. Our non-Christian friends live free of this particular type of pain.

Cast your mind back to Sunday morning. How many parents come to church with a broken heart? How many feel crushed under a burden of guilt or failure? How many have given up hope that their prodigal child will ever return? There are probably more of you than you might first think.

You Are Not Alone

When we suffer as Christians, we're not alone. First, because God is the perfect shepherd who cares for his flock:

He tends his flock like a shepherd:
he gathers the lambs in his arms
and carries them close to his heart;
he gently leads those that have young. (Isaiah 40:11)

This perfect shepherd has placed under-shepherds over our churches to care for us. Jesus models what pastors are to do for their congregations:

> *I am the good shepherd; I know my sheep and my sheep know me—just as the Father knows me and I know the Father—and I lay down my life for the sheep.*
>
> *(John 10:14-15)*

But it is not just leaders who are to care. As we will discover later in this chapter, all Christians should be engaged in the ministry of mutual encouragement. When we have had a bad week, church should be a haven of rest and a hospital for our wounded souls.

Sadly, this is not always the case. From time to time, I have referred to the pain of prodigal children in my preaching, and I have been surprised at some of the comments I have heard:

> *I'm so glad you mentioned that. I have never heard anyone speak about it before. I thought I was on my own.*
>
> *I would love to be able to pray with someone about this, but I don't have the courage to ask. I feel so bad. What would people think of me?*
>
> *I teach in the Sunday school, and I feel so ashamed that my kids aren't walking with the Lord. My kids grew up in the church, and people know them. I just keep quiet.*

We have already explored the fact that it is easy to feel confused or embarrassed or guilty when our children walk away from Jesus.

This can be compounded when people in the church know our children and want to find out how they're doing. What do we say?

Perhaps we're quite happy to ask people in the prayer meeting to pray for our neighbour or our work colleague or our team mate to be converted. But the people who are closest to us, the ones we pray for every day, often with tears, may never get a mention. This can lead to isolation. No one speaks about it, so we don't speak about it, so no one else speaks about it… and everyone feels alone. Instead of being honest, we wear a mask.

People Who Need People

I want to reaffirm that we don't need to do this on our own.

People need people. Relationships are necessary to our well-being. There's a song from an old musical which says that people who need people are the luckiest people in the world.[16] It would be more accurate to say that they are the *only* people in the world. We were made with an in-built need for friendship. This is why loneliness is such a curse. People of all ages suffer from it; agony aunts and uncles write about it; musicians sing about it.

I want to encourage you to take the mask off and share the burdens that you carry. Of course, this does not mean that everyone in the church needs to know. You don't have to share everything. But it could be something that you speak about in a home group or a prayer triplet. In one of the churches I served, there were a group of folk who joined together regularly to pray for their unconverted children. The prayer meeting was called "Parents in Pain". We didn't make great public announcements about it, but people knew that it took place and felt that it gave them permission to be honest.

We shouldn't feel guilty about seeking emotional support or spiritual wisdom or even professional help. Proverbs tells us:

For lack of guidance a nation falls,
but victory is won through many advisors.
(Proverbs 11:14)

The context of this proverb seems to be about the challenges of running a nation or fighting a war. But the principle is that seeking help from others is the way of wisdom. This certainly applies to the struggle with prodigal children. "Advisors" can give support or encouragement or counsel. It may be a mature Christian or a close friend or someone who has personal experience of a prodigal child.

So don't be afraid of sharing your concerns with your small group or prayer partners. If those aren't an option, ask your church leaders if they can direct you to a place or a person where you can find some help. Why not think of starting a prayer meeting for parents in pain?

There may be a special role for grandparents here. They have "skin in the game", as we say. If they're Christians, they're probably already praying for their grandchildren. Even if they're not Christians, they will want to give emotional support if the presenting issues concern the personal well-being of the child in question.

At the same time, do be aware that, whether it is with family or friends, we must respect the privacy of our children. It's probably not wise to speak to too many people about your concerns. If your child does return to church, they won't want to think that everyone has been talking about them or knows all the details of their circumstances. This is particularly the case when the issues concern gender or sexuality. Proverbs warns that "a gossip betrays a confidence" but commends "the prudent" who "hold their tongues" (Proverbs 20:19; 10:19)—so if the matter is not something that your child is sharing publicly, keep the circle of knowledge as tight as possible.

A Community of Encouragement

Finally, I want to speak a word to church family who are supporting parents in pain. After all, the church is at the centre of God's purposes in the world. The book of Hebrews tells us that as a result of the work of Christ, we have access into God's presence, and we can now…

> *… draw near to God with a sincere heart and with the full assurance that faith brings, having our hearts sprinkled to cleanse us from a guilty conscience and having our bodies washed with pure water.*
>
> *(Hebrews 10:22)*

But we do not do this on our own:

> *And let us consider how we may spur one another on towards love and good deeds, not giving up meeting together, as some are in the habit of doing, but encouraging one another—and all the more as you see the Day approaching. (v 24-25)*

Whenever we meet with our fellow Christians, we are to come with an agenda. We are to deliberately "consider" how to encourage each other. How can I spur on or stir up or provoke my fellow Christians to grow in love and to be rich in good deeds? We are to give "encouragement" so that our fellow Christians feel affirmed in their faith and are inspired towards love and good deeds. The Greek word which the author uses is rich in its implications. It can mean to warn, to urge, to comfort, to aid, to beseech.

It conveys the idea of coming alongside someone, helping them to be a better follower of Jesus even when they feel like giving up.

I remember once standing a few hundred yards from the finishing line of a half marathon. Next to me there was a young woman who seemed to know virtually every runner. As they came around the corner and approached the end of the race, she cheered them on:

Go on, Sam. You're almost there!

Well done, Emily. Just a few more metres!

Keep going, Raj. You're doing well!

I was amazed that she knew so many of the competitors, until it dawned on me that all she was doing was reading the names off their vests! Nonetheless, each runner appeared to respond with a fresh surge of energy. Words of encouragement change everything!

And so it is in the church as well. Take a moment to consider: What is your church doing to help people who are struggling with prodigal children? Do you rejoice with those who rejoice and mourn with those who mourn (Romans 12:15)? If your children are Christians, are you sensitive when you talk to someone whose children are not yet saved?

And a brief word to church leaders. As we have seen, this is a major pastoral issue, and church leaders cannot ignore it. We need to exercise particular sensitivity in this area. It is deeply emotional and often causes embarrassment.

Think about an occasion such as the baptism of a young person. We are right to rejoice! But how does this impact parents in pain? Is there something you could say, or give space to in your prayers, that would acknowledge that?

Consider the reception that people receive after they've been away for a while. Does your church welcome backsliders and prodigal children like the father in the parable, or do you resemble the older brother in his coldness and judgmentalism?

What about your general tone: do you approach the subject of suffering in a glib or simplistic way? It is quite easy to be triumphalist and give the impression that there's no room for parental pain. Do we create an atmosphere in which people feel free to share the things that are on their hearts?

These are all important questions for church leaders to consider.

Putting It into Practice

Paul encourages us to "carry each other's burdens, and in this way you will fulfil the law of Christ" (Galatians 6:2). But what does this look like in practice? Here are some ways in which every church member can support parents in pain:

- *Do* encourage people to talk, and learn to be a good listener. We often want to jump to quick answers, and the results are often unhelpful. So don't imagine that "one size fits all". Each situation is unique. You will discover this if you listen carefully and ask gentle questions.

- *Do not* belittle their pain. For many parents, this is almost the only thing they can think about. It trumps every other concern and sucks the joy out of life. Do your best to enter in to what they are feeling and show empathy.

- *Do* offer to pray—why not there and then? Ask them how you can best pray for them. Pray for the child's conversion but don't stop there. Pray with imagination, avoiding glib and clichéd phrases.

- *Do* admit when you don't have an answer. Admitting this doesn't mean that you have failed. They are probably not looking for answers anyway—what they are crying out for is someone to show compassion and empathy. So give them emotional support and show that you care.

- *Do* be ready to offer an alternative perspective. This is particularly true if they are bearing a heavy weight of guilt. Help them to recognise the difference between true and false guilt. If it is false guilt, they can ignore it; if it is genuine guilt, they can repent and know forgiveness.

- *Do* give spiritual support by pointing them to Jesus. This is by far the best thing that you can do for any other Christian, whatever their circumstances. The Bible encourages us to keep our eyes firmly fixed on him (Hebrews 12:1-3). This may not remove the problem, but it will help us to persevere.

- *Do* offer real hope. You might like to point them to some of the verses that we referred to in earlier chapters. You cannot give them the false assurance that their child will definitely be saved, but you can give them real hope and encourage them to persevere in prayer.

- *Do* share the comforts that you have received from God. When God allows us to suffer, one of his purposes is to enable us first to receive comfort from himself and then to offer that same comfort to others (2 Corinthians 1:3-7). So point them to the Bible verses that have helped you and share your own experience of God's comfort.

Picture again your church on a Sunday. The last song has been sung, and the benediction has been pronounced. There may be a moment of silence, but then people begin to leave their seats. What will you see?

Sure, some people are making a quick exit or rushing to collect children from Sunday school. Others are engaged in deep conversation with the person next to them. But what I most love to see is people in twos or threes praying together. Perhaps God spoke in some specific way during the service. What I would love to think is that in that intimate moment among people that we know and love, we can open our hearts and share those things that cause us most pain—including our concern for our prodigal children.

QUESTIONS

1. The Bible uses shepherding as a picture of the way in which we can help and encourage each other, including parents in pain. Look again at Isaiah 40:11 and John 10:14-15 and compare them with Psalm 23. What do we learn from these verses about the ways in which we can help support and encourage each other?
2. What are the reasons why we might try to live our Christian life in isolation? Is there anything preventing you from sharing your deepest concerns with your fellow Christians?
3. This chapter also warned against breaking confidences and sharing too much about our children. Do you think you're in danger of that? How would you know where the line is?
4. How can we best go about creating a culture of encouragement in the local church? What are the barriers we need to overcome? In what practical ways can we stimulate mutual encouragement?
5. Look at the list of suggestions at the end of the chapter. How could you put them into practice? What would you add to this list?

EPILOGUE

Sometimes God keeps us waiting.

I mentioned in a previous chapter that when I was first converted, my greatest longing was that my parents might be saved. I prayed for them every day, and during my second term at university, my dad became a Christian. He was 50 years old, and he followed Christ faithfully for the next ten years before the Lord took him to heaven. One of the last things Dad asked me to do was to keep praying for my mum because he wanted to see her in heaven.

But Mum was resolutely closed to the gospel. She was the kindest and most generous woman I have ever met, but as my dad got closer to God, she seemed to get further away. She came to church for my dad's funeral but was adamant that she would never go to church again. We occasionally talked about my faith, but the conversations grew rarer, and it seemed that she would never come to Christ. I prayed for her for almost 50 years, but still she held out.

Then she became ill. She had beaten cancer, but now it seemed that her heart was failing. With fear and trepidation,

I went to see her. She looked so tiny and helpless in the bed. I held her hand and told her that I loved her.

Then I asked:

Mum, do you know where Dad is?

Yes. He's in heaven, isn't he?

Yes Mum. Do you know how he got there?

No.

Would you like me to tell you?

In the past she might well have she said that she wasn't interested, but this time she said:

Yes please. I think I would.

So I told her about Jesus. I read the story of the thief on the cross who came to trust in Jesus right at the end of his life. I told her that he went to heaven not because he was good but because Jesus died for sinners. My dad had trusted Jesus, and that was why he was in heaven.

For a few moments there was silence, and then she said:

Do you think that I could become a Christian?

Of course!

Holding my mum's hand, I led her to Christ. Amazingly, she didn't die, and at the first opportunity she went to church. She lived into her 90s and gave clear evidence of a transformed life.

I've told you this story because I want to encourage you to continue to pray for your unsaved children. I prayed for my mum for almost 50 years. I prayed for lots of things for her, but in particular I prayed for her to become a Christian. Were there times that I almost gave up? Yes! Were my prayers powerful and eloquent? Absolutely not! Was I convinced that one day she would come to faith? Probably not.

But in spite of my small, feeble faith, God heard and answered.

So keep praying and don't give up. It would be great to see your children converted before the Lord takes you to heaven. But maybe you will be like my dad, who never saw his wife's conversion but now rejoices with her in the presence of Christ.

Sometimes God keeps us waiting. But even that is part of his plan. When our human strength fails and our hopes grow dim, we can turn to the one who gives strength to those who are weak, and rejoice in his promises:

> *He gives strength to the weary*
> *and increases the power of the weak.*
> *Even youths grow tired and weary,*
> *and young men stumble and fall;*
> *but those who hope in the LORD*
> *will renew their strength.*
> *They will soar on wings like eagles;*
> *they will run and not grow weary,*
> *they will walk and not be faint. (Isaiah 40:29-31)*

Keep going. Don't give up!

ENDNOTES

1 Max Lucado, *No Wonder They Call Him the Savior* (Multnomah Press, 1986), p. 158-159.

2 *Confessions* 13:1:20, Loeb Classical Library, p. 37.

3 Quoted in the frontispiece of Steven Pinker, *The Better Angels of Our Nature: A History of Violence and Humanity* (Penguin, 2012).

4 Edward H. Joy, "All your anxiety, all your care", 1929.

5 I picked up this neat threefold statement from several sermons by Vaughn Roberts.

6 See, for example, *Does the Bible Affirm Same-Sex Relationships? Examining 10 Claims About Scripture and Sexuality* by Rebecca McLaughlin (The Good Book Company, 2024).

7 Help and resources can be found from organisations such as True Freedom Trust (truefreedomtrust.co.uk), Living Out (www.livingout.org) or Harvest USA (harvestusa.org).

8 For examples of both of these, see *Born Again This Way: Coming Out, Coming to Faith, and What Comes Next* by Rachel Gilson (The Good Book Company, 2020).

9 I have used this anecdote before in a book specifically addressing the problem of suffering: Paul Mallard, *Invest Your Suffering* (IVP UK, 2013).

10 Scholars identify both individual psalms of lament (e.g. Psalm 3; 6; 13; 22; 28; 25; 31; 56; 57; 71; 77; 86; 142) and communal psalms of lament (e.g. Psalm 12; 44; 60; 74; 79; 80; 85; 90).

11 Mark Vroegop, *Dark Clouds, Deep Mercy* (Crossway 2019), p. 16.

12 Jerry Bridges, *Trusting God, Even When Life Hurts* (NavPress, 2008). p. 214.

13 Kevin DeYoung, *The Hole in our Holiness* (Crossway 2012), p. 47.

14 John Stott, *Guard the Truth: The Message of 1 Timothy and Titus*, The Bible Speaks Today (InterVarsity Press, 1996), p. 98.

15 Those who commit suicide have usually been struggling with depression or other serious mental issues. They are not thinking in a clear way, and suicide seems to be the only way out. Suicide and self-harm are sinful and can never be appropriate Christian responses to the trials of life. However, we cannot assume that this proves that a person was never saved in the first place—nor that suicide is unforgivable for those united to Christ. As in the other cases described above, we have to leave our child in God's hands and not come to unfounded conclusions about their ultimate destiny.

16 "People", composed by Jule Styne with lyrics by Bob Merrill for the 1964 Broadway musical *Funny Girl* and sung by Barbra Streisand.

thegoodbook COMPANY

BIBLICAL | RELEVANT | ACCESSIBLE

At The Good Book Company we are dedicated to helping Christians and local churches grow. We believe that God's growth process always starts with hearing clearly what he has said to us through his timeless and flawless word—the Bible.

Ever since we opened our doors in 1991, we have been striving to produce resources that are biblical, relevant, and accessible. By God's grace, we have grown to become an international publisher, encouraging ordinary Christians of every age and stage and every background and denomination to live for Christ day by day and equipping churches to grow in their knowledge of God, their love for one another, and the effectiveness of their outreach.

Call one of our friendly team for a discussion of your needs or visit one of our local websites for more information on the resources and services we provide.

Your friends at The Good Book Company

thegoodbook.com | thegoodbook.co.uk
thegoodbook.com.au | thegoodbook.co.nz